# From Captivity to Fame or
# The Life of George Washington Carver

## Raleigh H. Merritt

# FROM CAPTIVITY TO FAME
# OR THE LIFE OF
# GEORGE WASHINGTON CARVER

BY

## RALEIGH H. MERRITT

**MEADOR PUBLISHING COMPANY**
27 Beach Street
**BOSTON, MASSACHUSETTS**

COPYRIGHT, 1929 BY RALEIGH H. MERRITT
Raleigh Howard Merritt, was given permission
to compile and write this book, of which I
am the subject.
Signed George Washington Carver.
PRINTED IN THE UNITED STATES OF AMERICA
THE MEADOR PRESS, BOSTON, U. S. A.

## DEDICATION

To those who have worked so willingly to bring about good will and a better understanding between the races, through co-operation in promoting industry and thrift, this book is dedicated.

R. H. M.

# PREFACE

The purpose of this book is to record the eminent achievements of a great agricultural chemist, Dr. George Washington Carver, of the Tuskegee Institute; to make known his interesting childhood and youth, his early struggles and later triumphs; and also to accompany him into the great creative stretch of thirty-three years at the Tuskegee Institute, during which time he has accomplished so much for the betterment of mankind.

This book shows him deeply plunged into work for which he has always had an indubitable capacity; it reveals the exercise of his unsurpassed ability, his keen reasoning powers, and his 'uncommon' common sense. He is shown at work in his laboratory, reaching out into all regions of science and nature. He is also shown painting flowers, one of his pastime hobbies.

Finally, he has emerged triumphantly from countless difficulties, bringing with him hundreds of by-products from the peanut, the sweet potato, the pecan; and also paints, stains and dyes from common clays of the South--the fruits of victorious struggles.

The supplementary section of this book is composed of bulletins on food and food subjects etc., issued by Dr. Carver. I should think that a few of them will be of especial value to the house-wife, and also the farmer.

While studying agriculture at Tuskegee, I was brought into somewhat intimate relations with Dr. Carver, and began an acquaintance which has continued to grow. Like all students who come in contact with him, I learned to regard him not only as a kindly and good-natured teacher, but also as one who radiated fatherly love. It occurred to me that some day I should like to put something in book form about his life and his marvelous accomplishments.

I make no attempt, however, to give a complete account of Dr. Carver's life and works. I should think this would not be possible. Only certain incidents can be detailed with accuracy.

Conscious of my limitations as a biographer, I have desired only to make this volume a fair sketch of a remarkable and extraordinary man.

Dr. Carver prefers not to be made the subject of any biography. He has felt, however, that if it is to be written, it is best done by a friend who has known him for several years, and whose judgment and discretion he can trust, and one who, because of his knowledge of the facts, will not misrepresent him.

I wish to express my appreciation and thanks to Professor A. Mack Falkenstein, of the Drexel Institute, for suggestions and assistance he has so willingly given me in the preparation of this volume; and also Mr. Orrin C. Evans, Feature Editor, of the Philadelphia Tribune. I am also most grateful to Mr. R. C. Atkins, Director of the Agricultural Department, of the Tuskegee Institute for several pictures which he so kindly placed at my disposal for this book. I am especially grateful to Dr. Carver, for portraits of himself and other pictures which he allowed me to use, and also for much material he placed at my disposal. I am thankful to Mr. Julius Flood, of Tuskegee Institute, for pictures and other material which he was so generous to send me; I am also deeply appreciative to Miss Abigail Richardson for one cut of Dr. Carver.

I am very grateful to the following for material which was reproduced in this book: J. L. Nichols & Company; the Black Dispatch; The Tuskegee Messenger, by courtesy of Mr. Albon L. Hosley; The Highland Echo, by Mr. Robert T. Dance, of Maryville College, Tenn.

I am very grateful, indeed, to everyone who so generously responded to my request in submitting statements of views and comments on Dr. Carver's Life and Works. It would take up too much space to mention each one by name.

RALEIGH HOWARD MERRITT,

December 31, 1928.
Philadelphia, Pa.

# CONTENTS

- I. Birth and Early Childhood . . . . .
- II. Early Schooling and Struggles . . . . .
- III. Working His Way Through College . . . . .
- IV. First Twelve Years at Tuskegee . . . . .
- V. Discovers Possibilities of Native Products . . . . .
- VI. The Tuskegee Farmers' Conference . . . . .
- VII. His Creative Ability . . . . .
- VIII. The Carver School Farm Club . . . . .
- IX. Still Achieving and Helping People . . . . .
- X. Views and Comments . . . . .

# SUPPLEMENT

- XI. 105 Different Ways to Prepare the Peanut for the Table . . . . .
- XII. The Sweet Potato and Various Ways to Prepare It . . . . .
- XIII. How to Make and Save Money on the Farm . . . . .
- XIV. How to Raise Pigs with Little Money . . . . .
- XV. Poultry Raising . . . . .
- XVI. The Tomato . . . . .
- XVII. The Cow Pea . . . . .
- XVIII. Three Delicious Meals Every Day . . . . .
- XIX. 43 Ways to Save the Wild Plum Crop . . . . .
- XX. Alfalfa . . . . .
- XXI. The Pickling and Curing of Meat in Hot Weather . . . . .

# LIST OF ILLUSTRATIONS

- George Washington Carver . . . . . Frontispiece
- The Creamery at Tuskegee . . . . .
- Dr. Carver Painting . . . . .
- Dr. Carver at Work in His Laboratory . . . . .
- Another View of the Laboratory . . . . .
- Experiment Station Work--Results of Soil Improvement . . . .

- Exhibit of Milk and Cream Made from Peanuts . . . . .
- Sketch of Tuskegee Institute Farm . . . . .
- The Institute Truck Garden Exhibit . . . . .
- A Group of Representative Progressive Farmers . . . . .
- Members of the Carver School Farm Club . . . . .
- Silver Cup Presented Dr. Carver by North Carolina Negro Farmers Congress . . . . .
- Tuskegee Institute Swineherd . . . . .

**From Captivity to Fame**

## CHAPTER I.

## BIRTH AND EARLY CHILDHOOD

The romantic rise of George W. Carver, is a marvelous occurrence in the history of great Americans. He was born in a crudely constructed log cabin on the farm of one Moses Carver, (a German) near Diamond Grove, Missouri, during the dark days of emancipation in 1864. Out of poverty and obscurity this little boy was destined to become an outstanding representative of his race; an apostle of good will between the races; a creative genius, and one of the greatest scientists the world has ever known.

The reader will not be burdened with remarks regarding the research of George Carver's ancestry. He knew nothing about his ancestors himself, except what little he heard of his parents. He only knew that they were slaves, and that Moses Carver was the owner of his mother, and a neighboring slave-holder was the owner of his father.

## KIDNAPPED.

Probably the first and most spectacular occurrence in the life of this little boy was, when he and his mother were kidnapped by a gang of night-riders, and carried into Kansas. Although he does not remember anything about this, as he was only a baby about six weeks old.

Mr. Carver, his former master, sent out a rescuing party, which recovered him in exchange for a race horse valued at $300 part of the kidnapping force had gone ahead and carried the little boy's mother away. He never knew what became of her. He heard that his father was killed accidentally by an ox team while hauling wood. This is all he ever knew about his parents.

There were faint hopes of raising the babe of six weeks old, because he was very sickly, and had a severe whooping cough. Notwithstanding this, Mr. and Mrs. Carver adopted him into their family where he remained until he was about ten years old.

This little boy got his name in a very unusual way. He was not so fortunate as to inherit a name, but because of his faithful devotion to his work, and also his habitual truthfulness about everything, the Carvers called him George Washington. He got the name Carver from the Carver family. He speaks of Mr. Carver as being a very humane man.

George began to seek knowledge at an early age. During the day he spent almost all of his time roving the woods, and acquainting himself with every queer flower and every peculiar weed. He was also interested in studying the rocks, and different stones, and the birds. He usually played by himself as his playmates were very few.

As the manifestation of his love for the plants grew daily, the boy began to ask questions; "God, why did you make this plant, and for what purpose did you make it?" He felt that it was his duty to find out the use of these plants, which the great Creator placed here for man.

Moving pictures or 'movies' were unknown to George. But he got his share of amusement in listening to the birds sing. In fact, this was a great source of inspiration and encouragement to him. It was his highest ambition to finish his work as quickly as possible each day, so that he could get out into the woods among the things he loved best. Unconsciously he would find himself trying to tone his voice like that of the birds, either by whistling or singing.

One finds in him today countless echoes of the voices that spoke to him amidst the woods and hills of Missouri, during his boyhood days, the foundations of his character date from his earliest childhood. While he seemed just an average boy, yet he showed an unusual interest in the vital things of life.

He was frail and weak, therefore, he couldn't do very heavy work. But he usually made himself useful around the house by getting wood and bringing in chips and seeing to it that the fires were kept going. Occasionally he went to the spring for a pail of water, this being the chief source of water supply for the house, as was common in those days. There was nothing more thrilling and inspiring to George, than listening to the chirping of the birds, the humming of the bees, and the rhythmic echoes of the brooks and rills which seemed to have been repeating the sounding joy of Nature's blessings on a bright and sunny spring day, as he climbed the hills on his homeward journey.

It was during those days that the qualities which are essential to surmount obstacles, were unconsciously woven into the fiber of his character. These characteristics have followed him through life.

Among the things George did around the place was to assist Mrs. Carver prepare meals for the family. He soon learned to be a first class cook. He even learned to sew and mend clothes. After each meal George made himself useful by washing the dishes and getting the kitchen and dining room in order. After finishing his work he would hasten to the woods to play. He busied himself in the woods, gathering bunches of flowers, and sometimes he would fill his pockets with rocks, and sometimes with bugs. He formed such a habit of this that Mrs. Carver used to force him to turn out his pockets before she would allow him to come in the house.

An incident occurred one day which George has never forgotten. Mr. Carver usually went to town twice each year, and George usually went with him on every other trip. The time came for Mr. Carver to go to town, and it happened not to be George's time to accompany him, so he had to remain at home and see that all the livestock were properly cared for and fed that night. It occurred to George, however, that this was the time to play. He seemed to have enjoyed himself as never before. His enjoyment was so great, apparently, that he couldn't concentrate on his duties, so he forgot to feed the stock before night came. After nightfall came, however, he recalled that he hadn't discharged his all-important duty.

Realizing that it was about time for Mr. Carver to return from town, George hastily rushed to accomplish his task and thereby avert a whipping which he knew was the next thing he would get if he had neglected to do his work. By this time it was too dark for him to see without a light. The first thing he thought of was to get the parlor lamp, light and use it, then put it back in its place before Mr. Carver came. But Mr. Carver returned before he had finished feeding the stock, and gave George a whipping for using that most "valuable lamp." The lamp is an old tin frame, round in shape, and has a socket or holder in which a candle was placed. The lamp gave a very dim light, but it didn't fail to furnish plenty of smoke. Such a lamp, however, was very rare and was considered something fine and out of the ordinary, in those days.

Dr. Carver has that old lamp today, and also an old spinning wheel which his mother used to spin flax, during the days of slavery on the plantation. He also has several other collections which he got during his boyhood days.

When I asked Dr. Carver about the date of his birth he said, "I should like to know the exact date of my birth myself, but I do not. As a rule no records of children from slave parents were kept. I suffered from this same custom."

Young Carver used to study an old blue-back speller by the dim light of the burning logs in the fire place. It was in this way that he learned this little book by heart.

He was a boy of quiet temperament, and poor health, and remained very small until he was about twenty years old. He showed no signs of future eminence. But the manifestations of his mental qualities are traceable back to his early boyhood days. No longer than last fall, in an address at Tulsa, he said, "We must disabuse our people of the idea that there is a short cut to achievement. Life requires thorough preparation; veneer isn't worth anything." He lived, as he does now, close to the things which are eternally true. It was in this manner that he learned his greatest lessons-- which have followed him through life and enabled him to be the man he is today.

Carver has walked the one straight path from boyhood. He always made it his aim to build on solid logic and facts. He always made every action be directed to some definite object. He was a 'dreamer'--a 'dreamer' who makes dreams become actualities by perseverance and hard work.

At an early age he was religiously inclined. One finds in him today these same inclinations. To him there is no conflict between science and religion.

As George was constantly in poor health, Mr. and Mrs. Carver thought it would be the best thing for him to prepare himself for work which would not require a great deal of physical exertion. They were entirely willing for him to go wherever he could get an education. This was about all the encouragement he got.

He never had the opportunity of attending Sunday school, in fact, he had no schooling, either secular or religious, except that he had learned from the little blue-back speller.

Under all unfavorable circumstances, George never became discouraged. He had a vision and an insight into the need of doing something for human betterment--particularly his race, which needed help and guidance in overcoming a tremendous handicap.

## CHAPTER II.

## EARLY SCHOOLING AND STRUGGLES.

It appears that George had a continuous desire of acquiring knowledge, even though no one encouraged him to enter school, after he had learned to master the blue-back speller by himself. From his limited source of information, however, he was not able to find answers to queries which were constantly pressing upon his mind. Therefore, he became displeased with present conditions.

During this time, he heard of a little school, which was about eight miles away. Finally, George decided to venture upon the journey to this school, although he was only ten years old. Mr. and Mrs. Carver had no objection to his leaving, as they wanted him to get an education, even though they gave him no financial assistance.

George set out on his journey to the little school at Neosho, a distance of eight miles of trudging over hills, through swamps and sandy bottoms; as the sun began fading behind the Western horizon he lost no time in trying to make his destination. As night drew near, he heard the whipporwill's cry, which was startling, and made him feel somewhat nervous as he became conscious of the responsibilities which he was assuming.

After arriving to Neosho, young Carver was confronted with countless obstacles and difficulties. In the first place, he was absolutely without financial means, he didn't have so much as a single penny; and in the second place, he didn't know anyone there, therefore, he had no place where he could spend the night.

George spent the first few nights in an old horse barn. After looking around for a short while he succeeded in getting odd jobs here and there for a make-shift livelihood. During the meanwhile he continued to make his stopping place in the old barn. Notwithstanding all of this hardship the boy entered school and continued to stick there.

Finally, he made friends with a Mr. and Mrs. Watkins, who adopted him into their family. They allowed him to attend school for what he could do in their home. He said, "Indeed, Mr. and Mrs. Watkins treated me as if I were a member of their family."

The school was taught by one teacher who was very poorly prepared. The school building was an old log cabin, poorly ventilated, and afforded but little protection from the wrath of the weather. The benches were so very high until the pupils' feet wouldn't reach the floor when sitting on them, and besides this, they (the benches) didn't have any backs on which the pupils could rest. School apparatus were unknown there, in fact, every inconvenience that imagination can paint existed.

It was here at this little crudely constructed school, however, that young Carver's ambition was kindled as never before. It was the latent qualities of the boy which were responsive, under the slightest favorable environment. Within a year he had mastered what this school had to offer.

## ON TO FORT SCOTT.

After completing the course which he had been studying during the past year, George was anxious to go wherever he could enter school. While wandering along the road, a mule team came along en route to Fort Scott, Kansas. Young Carver asked the people to let him go along with them, and they kindly allowed him to go. As it took several days to make the journey he was almost completely worn out when the team arrived at its destination.

Immediately after arriving to Fort Scott, George began to search for work. It was not very long before he had succeeded in getting a job as kitchen man and dishwasher. In fact, he did all kinds of house work, from cleaning rugs to cooking and house cleaning. The previous training he had gotten while with the Carvers made him efficient to master this new situation.

## ENTERS SCHOOL

While in Fort Scott, for a short time, young Carver entered school, although he continued to stick to his work. His stay in Fort Scott was marked with a continuous upward climb through difficulties and obstacles, attending school whenever possible, and in the meanwhile doing some kind of work to make ends meet.

There were no signs that he would merit high honors or future greatness. Obviously, we find qualities of self control, serious attention and concentration to his duties, and that which was eternally essential.

For months at the time, George was not able to buy a one cent postage stamp. Notwithstanding this fact, he never charged very much for his work he made a rule of charging a reasonable price for whatever he did for the people. It mattered not how badly he was in need, he never would accept any financial assistance from anyone. He never desired to make himself an object of pity, he only asked for a square deal in every particular.

After being in Fort Scott about seven years George returned to his old home place, to visit Mr. and Mrs. Carver. Being unusually small for his age he was able to go on half fare; the train conductor hesitated, however, to take him, because he thought that the boy was too small to make the trip alone. He made the trip, however, without any difficulty.

Mr. and Mrs. Carver were very glad to see George, as they had not seen him for several years. It took several days for him to tell them about his journey in Kansas. He told them how he had been struggling to keep in school, and also about his plans to go through college. They seemed to have been interested in everything he had to tell them.

George spent the entire summer with the Carvers. When he returned to Kansas he took with him the old polar lamp, and also an old spinning wheel which his mother used in spinning flax, on the plantation, during the days of slavery. He has both the spinning wheel and the old lamp now, which he values very highly.

After returning to Fort Scott, he set out to get things working. He opened a small laundry. As he knew the art of the business he succeeded in catering to the people in the neighborhood. He always did very fine work, and at reasonable rates. He gained the good will of the people in the community.

George grew with great rapidity during the period of two years. When he was about nineteen years old he was very frail and small, but by the time he was twenty-one he was about six feet tall.

After completing the high school course in Fort Scott, he began to make plans to enter college. He heard of an educational institution in Iowa. After communicating with the school he filed an application and sent it by mail. His application was accepted, he set out for the school soon afterward. After he arrived on the scene, however, the president of the school refused to admit him, because he was a Negro. The boy had spent nearly all the money he had for car fare in getting there.

After being refused admittance to this school, he soon found himself without enough money to get out of the town. He began to seek for a job at once. Finally be succeeded in getting a few carpets to clean, soon afterward, however, he got a job as cook, and he continued at this until he had earned enough money to open a laundry. It was not long before his little business was patronized by students from the school, and also people in the immediate community. He remained there, however, until the following spring. Then he went to Winterset, Iowa, where he served as a first class cook in a large hotel.

After being there for some time he attended a church, (for white people) one evening. He took a seat in the rear of the building, but when the choir and congregation sang, he found himself taking an active part in singing. He evidently had a beautiful voice, because the soprano soloist of the choir, Mrs. Millholland was very favorably attracted by his voice. Mr. Millholland came to the hotel the next evening and inquired for George, and he invited young Carver to his home to sing for Mrs. Millholland and himself.

After arriving at Mr. and Mrs. Millholland's home George sang while Mrs. Millholland played. She was kind enough to have George come up once each week for vocal instruction.

Mr. and Mrs. Millholland became staunch friends of George. He used to tell them about the many things he had to do during the day, and also about his plans to continue his schooling. They always listened to him with great interest, and encouraged him to go on with his education. They also encouraged him to cultivate his artistic ability. He could paint very well. It is said that one of his paintings at the World Fair at Chicago, was valued at four thousand dollars.

Not long afterwards he made his way to Simpson College, at Indianola, Iowa, where he registered for the regular course, and took music, on the side, and also did some work in art.

When he had paid his entrance fee he had exactly ten cents left. With this small amount he invested it into five cents worth of corn meal and five cents worth of suet, and he lived an entire week on this menu.

Providently, a way was opened by the time his small supply of foods had exhausted. It was not long, however, before another turning point took place. His instructor was profoundly impressed with his talents and his ability. But he frankly told George that there was not much that he could hope for there, in the way of developing his talents.

Young Carver left Simpson College, and made another effort to accumulate something so that he could enter the Iowa State College, at Ames.

I have a letter from Dr. John L. Hillman, President of Simpson College, relative to Dr. Carver's record when he was a student there. Dr. Hillman says: "He was a student at Simpson College for three years. He took his degree in Agriculture at State College at Ames, and gave such promise that he was retained for some time on the faculty there until he was called to Tuskegee Institute.

"When I consider the difficulty with which he had to contend, I am simply amazed at what he has accomplished. His spirit and character are even more wonderful than his accomplishments.

"Our College conferred upon him the honorary degree of Doctor of Science last commencement, June 1928."

This picture shows two students engaged at work in the creamery. This creamery has modern equipment, and the management employs a large force of students, who get practical experience by working, and at the same time earn something to defray expenses while in school.

Tuskegee and the entire community are served with milk from this creamery every morning, just as people are served in large cities.

This picture shows two students engaged at work in the creamery. This creamery has modern equipment, and the management employs a large force of students, who get practical experience by working, and at the same time earn something to defray expenses while in school.

Tuskegee and the entire community are served with milk from this creamery
every morning, just as people are served in large cities.

# CHAPTER III.

# WORKING HIS WAY THROUGH COLLEGE

By working hard and economizing closely young Carver saved a small sum of money, with which he entered Iowa State College, at Ames, in 1890, where he began the study of agricultural chemistry. Indeed, life at college with him was very much like that of his early boyhood days, in that it was marked with constant struggles in making ends meet. That is, he had to do something for a livelihood while attending school.

After getting to College and qualifying to enter he was soon confronted with the question of finding lodging accommodation on the campus. This embarrassment, however, marked the beginning of a life time friendship between young Carver and Professor James Wilson, then Director of the Agricultural Experiment Station. After hearing about Carver being refused a place to stay, Professor Wilson said, "George may stay in my office." He proved to be a real friend to young Carver and did whatever he could to assist him.

Several years after the occurrence of this incident, when Carver had become Director of Agriculture at the Tuskegee Institute, his old friend, Professor Wilson, was visited to Tuskegee. To both this occasion was an exchange of reminiscence of the past days at the Iowa State College. At this time the former Professor of agriculture had arisen to the Secretaryship of the United States Department of Agriculture, a member of the President's Cabinet.

George did various odd jobs for a livelihood while in College. At times, however, he was without a penny, and for months he was not able to purchase a postage stamp. Notwithstanding this state of affairs he continued in college and applied himself to his studies. He always tried to do common things uncommonly well. He made it a rule to do his work so well that no one could come behind him and improve upon it.

One should not imagine that young Carver's life at college was all serious. Obviously he was always on the alert for everything pertaining to the essentials of life. Yet he was as fond of playing as a fellow could possibly be under the circumstances.

Carver took an active part in the various college activities. It is interesting for one to note how he had grown from a sickly boy to be a young man with good health, which made him physically fit as well as intellectually. Spending a great deal of his time outdoors, close to nature, and also throwing himself into various activities are the prime factors which made his success possible. He was not an athlete in the least sense, yet he knew how to make the most of any occasion.

Another thing which was peculiar about Carver, was that he would never accept any financial assistance from anyone, it mattered not how serious conditions got with him. He knew that he should train himself to have self-reliance, perseverance, courage and the knack of sticking to a thing to the finish.

Young Carver got a great deal of his education through observation, as well as from the text book. There was hardly anything that escaped his attention. He used to watch the ant and various insects, and made a very close study of them. It was from these insignificant insects that he learned great lessons--lessons which have enabled him to be a great servant for the people.

In applying himself while in college he sought to lay a brick in the foundation of his character each day, by making line upon line, precept upon precept, here a little and there a little, until he had become efficient for future service for human betterment. He followed his Star as was destined by his Great Creator.

While studying agriculture, Carver was placed in charge of the greenhouses. Here he made a close study of plant life, giving special attention to bacterial laboratory work in systematic botany. Young Carver's work was so satisfactory until he won the admiration of all of his teachers. He was often pointed out as a studious young man, with assiduous and sterling qualities. Carver earned enough by working in the greenhouses to pay his current expenses.

Another method by which he earned spending 'change' while in college, was that of selling lye hominy. That is, he would take corn and boil it in clear water, adding a little lye, which made the corn soft and also made it so that the outer coat of the corn would peel off after getting to the boiling stage. After this corn had cooked thoroughly and peeled, it was removed and washed thoroughly in clear water. Then it was removed again and seasoned to taste, after which it was fried or prepared in other forms. Young Carver always found a great demand for his lye hominy among the students. The small sums of money realized from the sales of his hominy helped greatly in putting him through college. In another chapter several ways are given for preparing lye hominy.

During the scholastic year of 1893-4 Carver began to look forward to getting himself permanently located for work, as he was to be graduated at the coming commencement. This matter was not worrying him, however, as he had given such promise during the four years there, that it had been intimated to him that he would be retained on the faculty of the State College after graduating. He continued to make the most of his work at the greenhouses.

His artistic ability, which was cultivated to some extent while at Simpson College, was greatly cultivated by practical work and experience while he was in charge of the flowers at the greenhouses. He studied flowers so closely until he learned to paint any design and variety with such touch that one could not distinguish his flowers from real ones, unless they were very closely examined. In another chapter of this book he is shown painting flowers, one of his past-time sidelines, during brief periods of a very busy life.

Carver graduated from State College in 1894, receiving his B. S. degree in agriculture. Sometime before commencement he was assured that he would be given work, so he began planning to enter upon his new field of labor.

Young Carver continued to pursue an advance course in the science of agriculture, taking this along with the bacterial laboratory work in systematic botany. In 1896 he received M. S. degree in agriculture.

A few days ago I received a letter from the President of Iowa State College and he said "As a College we feel proud of Dr. Carver. Some of the teachers are still here who were here when he was a student."

Carver had never found any work more congenial and within keeping of his calling, than that he had been doing after graduation. He liked to teach because he was very much interested in the work.

His life has been an inspiration and an encouragement to both young and old people--in fact to most people who ever heard about him.

When Carver was going through college, evidently he resolved to apply the words of the great immortal emancipator, Lincoln, that " 'I'll prepare myself and when my time comes I'll be ready.' " Thus it came about in the year 1896, an opportunity for him to work for the betterment of his people in the South, where a man of his talent and ability was so badly needed.

This occurrence took place when Tuskegee's famous founder, the late Dr. Booker T. Washington, was sending out inquiries to various schools and colleges throughout the country for prepared young men and women. George W. Carver, was recommended to Dr. Washington as being a young man who was thoroughly educated in all matters pertaining to agriculture.

Dr. Washington wrote Carver, and asked him to come to Cedar Rapids, Iowa, where he (Washington) was scheduled to deliver an address. Carver got ready and set out for Cedar Rapids, immediately. After arriving there it was not long before he met Dr. Washington, and had a conference with him. Carver agreed to go to Tuskegee and do whatever he could to advance the agricultural department of the Tuskegee Institute.

Even though he was very well satisfied with his work at the State College, he was desirous of going to Tuskegee because he thought that he could be of more service to his people. The young professor of agriculture was far-sighted enough to know that before him, at Tuskegee, lay a vast field of possibilities. Having these facts in mind, and a desire of working for the uplift of his people in the South, Carver began to prepare to leave for Tuskegee Institute.

This shows Dr. Carver as he appeared while on one of his paintings, one of his pastime side lines.

This shows Dr. Carver as he appeared while on one of his paintings, one of his pastime side lines.

# CHAPTER IV.

# FIRST TWELVE YEARS AT TUSKEGEE.

During the year of 1896, Professor Carver entered upon his work at the Tuskegee Institute. After being there for a short time he began to study conditions of the Agricultural Department; and also busied himself in making a general survey of the community. After ascertaining what needed to be done, he organized plans for the purpose of doing effective work.

When Professor Carver entered upon his work at Tuskegee the agricultural department was in its infancy. Funds had not been available to run it on large basis. The old agricultural building was not adequate to accommodate various purposes for which it was used. It was just about as crude in architectural construction as one should have expected, during the yearly years of the school, when it was facing one struggle after another for the lack of funds.

This state of affairs, however, offered no difficulties for Carver to entertain, in fact, he considered disadvantages as stepping stones to accomplish his task. He simply got on the job and made himself busy.

One of the first things he set out doing was that of getting the laboratory in workable condition. Indeed, this was not a small job, because nearly all the necessary equipment was lacking. Here an opportunity came for him to practice a lesson which he learned when a boy, that is, the lesson of carving something out of nothing. Moreover, the lesson of translating opportunity into achievement, and how to triumph over complex problems.

As the apparatus in the laboratory were not sufficient, he sent his students out to the alleys to gather old bottles, broken china, and bits of rubber and wire, out of which he made apparatus. Soon afterwards, however, his temporary fixtures were displaced, gradually, with new equipment.

# STUDYING AND MAKING USE OF THINGS AT HAND

Dr. Carver began to roam over the fields and the woods, in the community, with the purpose of making a study of different kinds of soils, and various plants etc. He usually took along his botany case to gather specimens which he carried back to make a study of in the laboratory.

The people in the community didn't know what to make of him when he was going through the fields and over the hills with his case, stopping here and there and gathering plants. All of this was strange to them. They thought, however, that he was a "root doctor." Several people came to him for treatment and for medicine.

Professor Carver has always aimed to make complete utilization of the native products, which grow so abundantly in the South. He emphasized the fact, that the farmer should study market conditions, as to supply and demand, co-operative marketing, and also a number of other things pertaining to this phase of the agricultural industry. He says that this is just as important as making a study of "building-up the soil" for greater production.

## THE TUSKEGEE EXPERIMENT STATION

The Experiment Station is a plot which contains nineteen acres of land. Throughout the year experiments are made methodically to ascertain the qualities of various kinds of soils and their possibilities of producing crops under certain conditions and adaptations.

The soil is of a very poor quality, ranging from coarse sand to fine sandy loan, and clay loam. If crops are grown successfully there, (and they are) there certainly should not be any doubt about growing good crops in other sections of Alabama, or any parts of the South, where the soil is more fertile.

"Building up" this Experiment Station, and making experiments with rotations of crops has been one of the outstanding phases of Dr. Carver's work during the first twelve years of his work at Tuskegee.

In 1897, his report showed that, with the best methods and

Dr. Carver is shown at work in his laboratory, extracting milk and various products from the peanut.

Dr. Carver is shown at work in his laboratory, extracting milk and various products from the peanut.

BOOKER T. WASHINGTON

abundant use of fertilizer, there was a net loss on the operation of $16.25. The next year, however, he worked the soil up to where the operation brought a net gain of $4.00. As he continued to improve the soil, the yield of the crops increased every year. In 1904, he produced eighty bushels of sweet potatoes per acre on a plot of ground, and also grew another crop on the same ground that year. The return was $75.00 per acre. In 1905 he raised a five-hundred-pound bale of cotton on this same soil.

## FERTILIZERS--BUILDING UP SOIL

Dr. Carver says the results of twelve years' work on the Experiment Station plots, and in the laboratory prove that we are allowing to go to waste an almost unlimited supply of the very kind of fertilizer the majority of our soils are most deficient in. I mean muck from the swamps and leaves from the forest.

"Three acres of our Experiment Station has had no commercial fertilizers put upon it for twelve years, but the following compost: 2/3 leaves from the woods and muck from the swamp (muck is simply the rich earth from the swamp). 1/3 barnyard manure.

## HOW TO MAKE THE COMPOST

"Two loads of leaves and muck are taken, and spread out in a pen. One load of barnyard manure is spread over this. The pen is filled in this way. It is either rounded over like a potato-hill, or a rough shed is put over it to turn the excess of water, so as to prevent the fertilizing constituents from washing out. It is allowed to stand this way until spring.

## WHEN TO MAKE THE COMPOST

"Being your compost heap now; do not delay; let every spare moment be put in the woods raking up leaves or in the swamps pilling up muck. Haul, and put in these pens. Do not wait to get the barnyard manure--you can mix it in afterward, or if you cannot get the barnyard manure at all, the leaves and muck will pay you many times in the increase yield of crops.

## HOW TO USE.

"Prepare the land deep and through. Throw out furrows with a middle-buster two-horse plow; put in the compost at the rate of 2 tons per acre, 2 1/2, where the land is very poor; plant right on top of this. Handle afterwards the same as if any other fertilizer had been used.

"Save all the wood ashes, waste lime, etc., and mix into this compost.

## RESULTS.

"As stated above, three acres of our experimental farm has no commercial fertilizer put upon it for twelve years. The land has been continually cropped, but has increased in fertility every year, both physically, and chemically, on no other fertilizer than muck compost and the proper rotation of crops.

"This year 282 pounds of lint cotton, 45 bushels of corn, and 210 bushels of sweet potatoes were made per acre, with no other fertilizer than above compost.

"Try this; it will take only one or two trials to convince you that many thousands of dollars are being spent every year here in the South for fertilizers that profit the user very little, while Nature's choicest fertilizer is going to waste."

## HELPING THE SOUTHERN FARMER.

Professor Carver's primary object has always been that of being the greatest assistance to the Southern Farmers; in helping them have better farms, and happier homes, with plenty of food raised on the farms, and also a surplus to sell. Thus that class of people could soon become property owners, tax payers and independent--a class of people that would be an asset to any state.

Thirty-nine different bulletins have been issued by Professor Carver, on food subjects, and scientific farming.

This picture shows Dr. Carver, actively engaged at work in his laboratory, which is one of the best equipped laboratories in the country.

This picture shows Dr. Carver, actively engaged at work in his laboratory,
which is one of the best equipped laboratories in the country.

Hundreds of these bulletins have been distributed throughout the South. As a result of this, his bulletins are used extensively in all sections of the country now. He told me that hardly a day passes that he does not get a letter asking for a number of them.

Professor Carver has made many tours through the Southern States, to make demonstrations of various by-products, and to explain their possibilities. He has been doing this, and distributing the bulletins with the sole purpose of answering questions and solving problems for the farmer. In fact, he has sought to give the farmer free information and be of the greatest assistance to him in every possible way.

"During

(1 Booker T. Washington, Story Of My Life and Work, pg. 213, J. L. Nichols & Company, Naperville, Ill.)

the earlier years of the school we found it difficult to get students to take much interest in our farm work. They wanted to go into the mechanical trades instead. "After the opening of the new agricultural building and the securing of Mr. Geo. W. Carver, a thoroughly educated man in all matters pertaining to agriculture, the Agricultural Department has been put upon such high plane that the students no longer look upon agriculture as a drudgery, and many of our best students are anxious to enter the Agricultural Department.

"We have demands from all parts of the South for men who have finished our courses in agriculture, dairying, etc., in fact, the demands are far greater than we can supply.

## FIRST TWELVE YEARS AT TUSKEGEE.

Any process that does not get the best possible results is wasteful to the degree that it falls short of perfection. Fertilizer could not be used with slave labor, as its use required care and judgment, and even whipping did not instill this common sense of reason into slaves. Therefore, under slave conditions land could be used for only a few crops, then it must be left to grow up in weeds and grass. This system of agriculture was very wasteful.

"In view of this situation it is safe to affirm that under such a system of agriculture the available cotton land would some time or other come to an end. What then? Would the South find new occupation for the slaves? There was no chance of this."

Tuskegee Institute has been a great factor in solving this problem. The primary object of its founder was not only for the betterment of his people, but for the uplifting of the entire South.

Not less interest has been manifested by Dr. Carver in this most worthy cause.

Experiment Station Work, an exhibit of a county fair showing the results of correct soil improvement methods, or how to build up worn out soils.

# CHAPTER V.

# DISCOVERS POSSIBILITIES OF NATIVE PRODUCTS.

Prior to the coming of the boll wevil, cotton was considered as being the chief money crop of the South. Even the smaller farmer depended on his cotton crop, from which he expected to realize some cash money in the fall. But as soon as the boll weevil began invading the cotton regions of the South, and almost completely destroying promising crops of cotton, (estimated to be worth thousands of dollars) the farmer was placed in an intricate position. That is, he was faced with the problems of destroying the weevil, if possible, or that of substituting a native crop, for which he could find a demand in the markets throughout the year.

To discover such a product as this simply meant that a great deal of investigation and research work had to be carried on. During this time Dr. Carver was constantly working on the common peanut, to see what possibilities were tied up in it. He had already extracted a variety of products from it.

In fact, Dr. Carver had already found that the peanut contained prime qualities of importance in a balanced diet, and essential for the proper nutrition of man and other animals.

To date he has extracted 202 different products from the peanut, yet he says that its possibilities are not exhausted by any means.

In another chapter 105 different ways are given to prepare the peanut for the table, according to Dr. Carver's recipes. This is from a household point of view, however, and has no bearing on the 202 different products which he extracted from the peanut.

# A PARTIAL LIST OF THE 202 PRODUCTS FROM THE PEANUT

Salted peanuts, mixed pickles, soap and soap-sticks, face powder, face bleach, washing powder, milk, as good as or better than cow's milk, several kinds of wood stains and dyes, an assortment of cheese, chocolate bars, instant coffee, breakfast food, caramels, butter, flour, meal, lard, axle grease, stock food, brittle, Scotch butter, wafers, kisses, bisque, sprouts, relishes, cheese filler, slave, tan remover, shampoo lotion and printer's ink.

## MAKING USE OF THE PEANUT

The peanut has been used extensively throughout the South, particularly so during the World War. As the people become more acquainted with its various uses the demand will probably exceed all previous records. Thus, the farmer can figure on a fair price for his crop. This will mean a great step in forwarding the agricultural industry of the South.

During the fall of 1917, it was interesting for one to have seen farmers coming to Tuskegee with wagons loaded with peanuts; nearly every farmer who lived in the adjacent districts to Tuskegee was growing peanuts. They found a ready market for their product at the Tuskegee Institute, even though several acres of peanuts were grown on the farms of the School. Oils and a variety of other articles were extracted from these peanuts under the direction of Professor Carver.

I recall an incident which occurred during this unusual period of the "rising tide" of the lowly "goober." It happened in connection with a car load of peanuts which was shipped to Tuskegee. Somehow the door of the car had been ripped open, and several bushels of peanuts poured out on the ground. Soon afterwards, however, it occurred that a force of officers were detailed from the Commandant's office, only to discover bags of peanuts in the boys' rooms. Meanwhile, however, Professor Carver was still bent on carving upwards of 176 different by-products from the peanuts which had not been devoured.

## THE SWEET POTATO.

It appears that the sweet potato comes second on Professor Carver's list. He has extracted a variety of 178 different articles from this common product. The sweet potato is universally recognized as an important product, its possibilities, however, are too little known.

Yes, this is milk and cream, and it is as good or better than cow's milk. This is the result of one of Dr. Carver's extractions from the common peanut.

Yes, this is milk and cream, and it is as good or better than cow's milk. This is the result of one of Dr. Carver's extractions from the common peanut.

Throughout the South the sweet potato is grown more or less on large scales. Professor Carver has worked day after day, and sometimes at night, to unravel mysteries which this common product contains. In view of the fact, that sweet potatoes are very easily grown, and require but little outlay in cash to put on the market, its possibilities as a commercial product is not to be questioned.

"A theory is a theory because it lacks facts," Professor Carver, avers. To utilize the common things at hand has always been his aim. In his work he has always sought to produce something which would be of practical use to the people.

### SWEET POTATO BREAD

Sweet potato bread is made for the students and teachers at Tuskegee, from Professor Carver's recipes. I had the opportunity of trying that bread for some time, and I found it to be the best I have ever eaten. Everybody says this about the sweet potato bread. It has become famous for its pleasing taste; it's somewhat spongy, soft and just a trifle sweet. Anyone desiring to try Professor Carver's recipes for making this bread may see chapter on Sweet Potatoes. How to make sweet potato flour, starch, sugar bread and mock cocoanut are also listed.

### A PARTIAL LIST OF BY-PRODUCTS FROM THE SWEET POTATO.

The following is a partial list of the 178 different by-products which Dr. Carver extracts from the common sweet potato: Flour, meal, starch, library paste, mock cocoanut, breakfast foods, preserved ginger, vinegar, ink, shoe blacking, coffee, chocolate compound, bisque powder, dyes, candies, rubber compound, stock food, molasses, wood fillers, carmels etc.

### MISCELLANEOUS PRODUCTS

Dr. Carver has extracted paints, stains and dyes from common clays of Alabama and Georgia. He has also gotten stains and dyes from scuppernongs.

The pecan has also yielded a number of different products. Anyone desiring information about these products may write to the Research and Experiment Station, Tuskegee Institute, Alabama.

## IMPORTANCE OF THE AGRICULTURAL INDUSTRY

Dr. Carver has always emphasized the importance of the great agricultural industry, from which the food supply of the Nation comes; he has spared no efforts in trying to help educate the people to appreciate this fact.

Probably one of the greatest problems which is now before the United States Congress is the "farm relief bills." This, at least, is evident of the fact that agriculture as a profession and as a science has received the attention which it merits, as the greatest and most important industry of the country.

"Burn down the cities and leave the farms and the cities will spring up again as if by magic; but destroy the farms and leave the cities and grass will grow in the streets of every city in this country," said William Jennings Bryan.

## REFUSES TO COMMERCIALIZE.

One of the most outstanding peculiarities of Dr. Carver is, that he refuses to commercialize on his work. One need not think that Dr. Carver is doing this for a name. In fact, he has a habit of depreciating himself, and that of underestimating the regard in which others hold him. He has never sought for popularity, even though he has merited international fame by his marvelous achievements for mankind.

## THE BOOKER T. WASHINGTON SCHOOL ON WHEELS

"The Booker T. Washington School on Wheels" is composed of a group of teachers (four or five) and a very large truck which is well equipped with apparatus which the teachers use in demonstrating scientific farming; methods of improving the home, and most of all the teacher of domestic science and a trained nurse play a very important part on the program of this work.

This group of teachers travel throughout the rural districts of South and Southwest Alabama; going from one community to another with the purpose of assisting the Farmer. As a result of this work farm life in these districts has become happier and more cheerful. It appears that the isoation which formerly existed has been greatly broken.

Dr. Carver has taken a very active part in this great movement of "The Booker T. Washington School On Wheels," which is under the direction of the Tuskegee Institute. Various products which he has extracted from the peanut and the sweet potato, and also from other native products, have been exhibited on the tours through these districts. Hence, the farmers in that section of the State have been fortunate in getting first hand information as to the possibilities of the common products. There is no telling just how far reaching this movement may become.

## APPEARS BEFORE UNITED STATES CONGRESS.

After appearing before the Ways and Means Committee. Dr. Carver was allowed fifteen minutes to speak to the members of the Congress, and explain the possibilities of the peanut and the sweet potato. It is said that some of the wisest Congressmen thought that the subject which Dr. Carver was about to present could very easily be examined and explained completely within fifteen minutes.

But after he began opening up his bags, and bringing out one thing after another, and meanwhile explaining in detail, he had grasped the Senators' attention and was arousing their interest. Realizing, however, that his allotted time of fifteen minutes was about out. Dr. Carver began to bring his subject to a close, only to be hurled at with shouts of amazements and hurrahs to, "Carry on, go on, don't stop." As Tuskegee's wizard continued to develop his theme, he had completely gripped his hearers spell-bound. But the continuity of his discourse was frequently broken by recurring applauses. After Dr. Carver had finished he looked at the clock only to find that he had occupied the floor one hour and forty-five minutes, before that great august body.

Dr. Carver's demonstration was unanimously approved, and also attracted wide attention throughout the country. He was heralded as a creative genius, as never before.

Dr. Moton said, "Professor George W. Carver, of the Tuskegee Experiment Station has made some very valuable contributions to the food propaganda. At the request of Dr. Davis Fairchild, of the United States Department of Agriculture, Professor Carver went to Washington and presented to a number of officials of the department, some demonstrations in his experiments with sweet potatoes, and as a result of this and other activities here at the Institute, Professor Carver's work has become widely known. He has distributed by request, hundreds of bulletins on food subjects; has spoken at various places in the South, and has contributed to many publications, especially on the subjects of food substitutes."

## EDISON MAKES AN OFFER TO HIM.

Thomas Edison, the world's great inventor, sent his personal representative to Tuskegee for the purpose of making Dr. Carver an offer to join his mighty forces as an assistance in his laboratories at Orange Grove, New Jersey.

When questioned about this offer, Dr. Carver said, there was not much information to be had, concerning the conference between Edison's representative and himself. He said, "You see, Mr. Washington placed me here nearly twenty-five years ago, and told me to let 'down my bucket,' so I have always tried to do that, and it has never failed to come up full of sparkling water." And he continued, "Mr. Washington is not with us any more in person, and I would not be true to this great cause if I should leave here."

Dr. Carver felt that his work at Tuskegee was so far from being complete so he humbly refused to accept Edison's offer. He felt highly honored, but he said that he didn't "feel worthy of the offer."

A small sketch of the Tuskegee Institute Farm, and also the pasture on which the dairy cows are grazing.

A small sketch of the Tuskegee Institute Farm,
and also the pasture on which the dairy cows are grazing.

## HIS PERSONALITY.

The average person would probably not be impressed with Dr. Carver, on first sight, as being a man of unusual ability and talents. I recall an incident of significance which occurred some years ago. Dr. Carver had been invited to speak and demonstrate his products in a meeting at the Academy of Music in Philadelphia. I prepared for him as he was to spend some time with me.

My landlady became somewhat nervous as she said, "That big man" was going to stop at her home. Early in the morning, about three o'clock, a friend of mine accompanied me to the station to meet Dr. Carver. After getting back to the house we retired until late that morning.

After getting breakfast ready, however, I rushed upstairs to have him come to breakfast, as she nervously poised to see a great giant with a stiff neck and high collar, and with a walking cane, who would come striding downstairs as a mighty oak, with an imposing spirit of self-importance. But she was very much surprised when she saw that unassuming, unselfish, and God-fearing man of three score years, upon whose countenance radiated the spirit of friendliness, peace and good will to all mankind. After meeting Dr. Carver she soon felt perfectly comfortable again. All of that nervousness disappeared.

She found Dr. Carver very interesting, so much until this breakfast resulted almost into a conference, we spent at least two hours at the table. He made an impression upon her which will probably linger forever. She often relates that story now to her friends. This is not the only occasion which Dr. Carver has made lasting friends in almost this same way.

A few years ago Dr. Carver was invited to speak and make a display of his products in a certain city in Texas. The people who made this invitation to Dr. Carver, had made an agreement with the manager of a large theatre to have Dr. Carver speak there, but the manager's wife informed them that she wouldn't permit a Negro to appear in that building. Finally, however, she was persuaded to allow the meeting to be held there. After Dr. Carver had finished making his demonstration of the various products, and also the impressive explanations of it, the manager and his wife were very much pleased and were profoundly impressed in every way. She asked Dr. Carver to be sure to come again and make a complete display of all of his products.

Dr. Carver has lectured to students and teachers of various institutions and colleges throughout the South and parts of the North, both to colored and white people. This takes somewhat an interracial aspect, as his tours have resulted in better understanding between the races. Although he never talks on the so-called "race problem. Dr. Carver always confines his efforts on his work.

A display of the Truck Garden during the Farmers' Conference at Tuskegee, December 7, 1928.

# CHAPTER VI.

# THE TUSKEGEE FARMERS' CONFERENCE

Dr. Carver's exhibits have been looked upon as one of the outstanding phases of the Tuskegee Negro Farmers' Conference, during the past thirty years.

The primary object of this conference is that of assisting the farmers in that section, or throughout the South, in every possible way. Dr. Carver has always been a factor in carrying out this plan of the late Dr. Washington.

1"From the time I first began working at Tuskegee, I began to study closely not only the young people, but the condition, the weak points and the strong points, of the older people. I was very often surprised to see how much common sense and wisdom these older people possessed, notwithstanding they were wholly ignorant as far as the letter of the book was concerned.

"About the first of January, 1892, I sent out invitations to about seventy-five of the common, hard-working farmers, as well as to mechanics, ministers and teachers, asking them to assemble at Tuskegee on the 23rd of February and spend the day in talking over their present condition, their help and their hinderances, and to see if it were possible to suggest any means by which the rank and file of the people might be able to benefit themselves.

"In the Conference, two ends will be kept in view, first, to find out the actual industrial, moral and educational condition of the masses; second, to get as much light as possible on what is the most effective way for the young men and women whom the Tuskegee Institute and other institutions are educating, to use their education in helping the masses of the colored people to lift themselves up.

"In this connection, it may be said that, in general, a very large majority of the colored people in the Black Belt cotton district are in debt for supplies secured through the 'mortgage system', rent the land on which they live, and dwell in one-room log cabins. The schools are in session in the country districts not often longer than three months, and are taught in most cases in churches or log cabins with almost no apparatus or school furniture.

"The poverty and ignorance of the Negro which show themselves by his being compelled to 'mortgage his crops,' go in debt for the food and clothes on which to live from day to day, are not only a terrible drawback to the Negro himself but a severe drain on the resources of the white man. Say what he will, the fact remains, that in the presence of the poverty and ignorance of the millions of Negroes in the Black Belt, the material, moral and educational interests of both races are making but slow headway.

"In answering to this invitation we were surprised to find that nearly four hundred men and women of all kinds and conditions came. In my opening address I impressed upon them the fact that we wanted to spend the first part of the day in having them state plainly and simply just what their conditions were. I told them that we wanted no exaggeration, and did not want any cut-and-dried or prepared speeches, we simply wanted each person to speak in a plain, simple manner, very much as he would if he were about his own family fireside, speaking to the members of his own family. I also insisted that we confine our discussion to such matters as we ourselves could remedy, rather than in spending the time in complaining or fault finding about those things which we could not directly reach. At the first meeting of this Conference we also adopted the plan of having these common people themselves speak, and refused to allow people who were far above them in education and surroundings take up the time in merely giving advice to these representatives of the masses.

"Very early in the history of these Conferences I found that it meant a great deal more to the people to have one individual who had succeeded in getting out of debt, ceasing to mortgage his crop, and who had bought a home and was living well, occupy the time in telling the remainder of his fellows how he had succeeded, than in having some one who was entirely out of the atmosphere of the average farmer occupy the time in merely lecturing to them.

"I will let no man drag me down so low as to hate him." This inscription is engraved on the statue of Dr. Booker T. Washington, which was one of his sayings, and a manifestation wrought through his labors.

The statue is a typical illustration of his pleading for a fair chance for an oppressed people; through education, industry and thrift.

This group is composed of representatives of progressive farmers from various states, attending the Annual Negro Farmers' Conference at Tuskegee Institute, December 1928. Certificate of Merit Men are:
Left to Right, J. S. Seale, Philadelphia, Mississippi; Chris Oliver and wife, Snowdown, Ala.; P. L. Anderson, Boley, Okla.; John C. Claybrooks, Simsboro, Ark.

This group is composed of representatives of progressive farmers from various states, attending the Annual Negro Farmers' Conference at Tuskegee Institute, December 1928. Certificate of Merit Men are:

**Left to Right, J. S. Seale, Philadelphia, Mississippi; Chris Oliver and
wife, Snowdown, Ala.; P. L. Anderson, Boley, Okla.; John C.
Claybrooks, Simsboro, Ark.**

---

"In the morning of the first day of the Conference we had many representatives from various parts as we had time in which to tell of the industrial condition existing in their immediate community. We did not let them generalize or tell what they thought ought to be or was existing in somebody else's community, we held each person down to a statement of the facts regarding his own individual community. For example, we had them state what proportion of the people in their community owned land, what proportion lived in one-room cabins, how many were in debt, the number that mortgage their crops, and what rate of interest they were paying on their indebtedness. Under this head we also discussed the number of acres of land that each individual was cultivating, and whether or not the crop was diversified or merely be confined to the growing of cotton. We also got hold of facts from the representatives of these people concerning their educational progress; that is, we had them state whether or not a school-house existed, what kind of teacher they had and what proportion of the children were attending school. We did not stop with these matters; we took up the moral and religious condition of the communities; had them state to what extent, for example, people had been sent to jail from their communities; how many were habitual drinkers; what kind of minister they had; whether or not he was able to lead the people in morality as well as in spiritual affairs.

"After we had got hold of facts, which enabled us to judge of the actual state of affairs existing, we spent the afternoon of the first day in hearing from the lips of these same people in what way, in their opinion, the present condition of things could be improved, and it was most interesting as well as surprising to see how clearly these people saw into their present condition, and how intelligently they discussed their weak points as well as their strong points. It was generally agreed that the mortgage system, the habit of buying on credit and paying large rates of interest, was at the bottom of much of the evil existing among the people, and the fact that so large a proportion of them lived on rented land also had much to do with keeping them down. The condition of the schools was discussed with equal frankness, and means were suggested for prolonging the school term and building school-houses. Almost without exception they agreed that the fact that so large a proportion of the people lived in one-room cabins, where there was almost no opportunity for privacy or separation of the sexes, was largely responsible for the bad moral condition of many communities.

"When I asked how many in the audience owned their homes, only twenty-three hands went up.

"Aside from the colored people who were present at the Conference who reside in the "Black Belt," there were many prominent white and colored men from various parts of the country, especially representatives of the various religious organizations engaged in educational work in the South, and officers and teachers from several of the larger institutions working in the South. There correspondents present representing such papers as the New York Independent, Evening Post, New York Weekly Witness, New York Tribune, Christian Union, Boston Evening Transcript, Christian Register, The Congregationalist, Chicago Inter-Ocean, Chicago Advance, and many others.

"At the conclusion of the first Conference the following set of declarations was adopted as showing the consensus of opinion of those composing the Conference:

"We, some of the representatives of the colored people, living in the Black Belt, the heart of the South, thinking it might prove of interest and value to our friends throughout the country, as well as beneficial to ourselves, have met together in Conference to present facts and express opinions as to our industrial, moral and educational condition, and to exchange views as to how our own efforts and the kindly helpfulness of our friends may best contribute to our elevation.

"First. Set at liberty with no inheritance but our bodies, without training in self-dependence, and thrown at once into commercial, civil and political relations with our former owners, we consider it a matter of great thankfulness that our condition is as good as it is, and that so large a degree of harmony exist between us and our white neighbors.

"Second. Industrially considered, most of our people are dependent upon agriculture. The majority of them live on rented lands, mortgage their crops for the food on which to live from year to year, and usually at the beginning of each year are more or less in debt for the supplies of the previous year.

"Third. Not only is our own material progress hindered by the mortgage system, but also that of our white friends. It is a system that tempts us to buy much that we would do without if cash was required, and it tends to lead those who advance the provisions and lend the money, to extravagant prices and ruinous rates of interest.

"Fourth. In a moral and religious sense, while we admit there is much laxness in morals and superstition in religion, yet we feel that much progress has been made, that there is a growing public sentiment in favor of purity, and that the people are fast coming to make their religion less of superstition and emotion and more a matter of daily living.

"Fifth. As to our educational condition, it is to be noted that our country schools are in session on an average only three and a half months each year; and Gulf States are as yet unable to provide school-houses, and as a result the schools are held almost out-of-doors or at best in such rude quarters as the poverty of the people is able to provide; the teachers are poorly paid and often very poorly fitted for their work, as a result of which both parents and pupils take but little interest in the schools; often but few children attend, and these with great irregularity.

"Sixth. That in view of our general condition, we would suggest the following remedies: (1) That as far as possible we aim to raise at home our own meat and bread; (2) that as fast as possible buy land, even though a very few acres at a time; (3) that a larger number of our young people be taught trades, and that they be urged to prepare themselves to enter as largely as possible all the various avocations of life; (4) that we especially try to broaden the field of labor for our women; (5) that we make every sacrifice and practice every form of economy that we may purchase land and free ourselves from our burdensome habit of living in debt; (6) that we urge our ministers and teachers to give more attention to the material condition and home life of the people; (7) that we urge that our people do not depend entirely upon the State to provide school-houses and lengthen the time of the schools, but that they take hold of the matter themselves where the State leaves off, and by supplementing the public funds from their own pockets and by building schoolhouses, bringing about the desired results; (8) that we urge patrons to give earnest attention to the mental and moral fitness of those who teach their schools; (9) that we urge the doing away with all sectarian prejudice in the management of the schools.

"Seventh. As the judgment of this Conference we would further declare: That we put on record our deep sense of gratitude to the good people of all sections for their assistance, and that we are glad to recognize a growing interest on the part of the best white people of the South in the education of the Negro.

"Eight. That we appreciate the spirit of friendliness and fairness shown us by the Southern white people in matters of business in all lines of material development.

"Ninth. That we believe our generous friends of the country can best aid in our elevation by continuing to give their help where it will result in producing strong Christian leaders who will live among the masses as object lessons, showing them how to direct their efforts towards the general uplifting of the people.

"Tenth. That we believe we can become prosperous, intelligent and independent where we are, and discourage any efforts at wholesale emigration, recognizing that our home is to be in the South, and we urge that all strive in every way to cultivate the good feeling and friendship of those about us in all that relates to our mutual elevation."


(Booker T. Washington, the Story of My Life and Work, part of Chap. VII, by J. L. Nichols & Company).

# CHAPTER VII.

# HIS CREATIVE ABILITY

Dr. Carver has taken elements from their accustomed associations and brought them into others where they have new and multiplied significance. It is in some such manner as this, that he has been able to accomplish such marvelous results in his scientific investigations. His creative ability has enabled him to dissociate some parts of the sweet potato, the peanut, and other common products, and in his research and experimental work rearranged and re-associated some of the fragments with others. The result is something new, something useful and wholesome for human consumption.

When we speak of Dr. Carver's creative ability we see him as a true pioneer. We see him as a path 'blazer' upon the field of new endeavors, preparing the way for others. We see him as one who creates something tangible and useful.

Dr. Carver has been called a genius, a great scientist, a man with queer ways, and what not, etc. It is probably no more than reasonable for the popular mind to think of him as being an analytic, emotionless person who leads an apparent remote life in seeking remote facts. He takes nothing for granted, however, satisfying himself with only facts and results. His processes art based upon the application of chemical discoveries which lie at the foundation of great enterprises.

Having these facts in view will probably lead the inquiring mind to ask "What manner of man is this?" "He creates what?" "New precedents, new rules or what?" Perhaps, but more important, he makes possible in the future, situations enriched with further possibilities, more comprehensive understanding, broader and fairer relations. Moreover, he is a great factor in the building of a new civilization.

The reasons why agricultural conditions in the South became different from those in the North were at first chiefly due to climate and the conditions of the soil. In the South, with its rich land and long, warm growing season, tobaccoproved almost at once to be a money-making crop. Rice and indigo, and later, sugar cane and cotton were found to be exceedingly profitable, especially when cultivated on a large scale. Commercial production of this sort required extensive cultivation, cheap labor, and sufficient capital to carry on operations.

When the gin was invented, cotton was produced only in Georgia and South Carolina. It soon spread north as far as Virginia, and by 1815 was being grown in Alabama and Mississippi. Cotton culture with slave labor was a most wasteful process because there was no rotation of crops and no use of fertilizers. Cotton was raised until the soil was exhausted; then the planter moved west to take up fresh land. This continuous movement added Louisiana, Texas, and Oklahoma to the 'cotton states', and was checked only when it was found that cotton would not grow successfully. Agricultural practice was very far from scientific.

Apparently the soil around Tuskegee was worn out during the days of slavery when the process of farming was careless, and not very much attention was given to the preservation of soil fertility.

When Professor Carver entered upon his work at Tuskegee, this worn out soil was one of the most serious problems which confronted him in his work. It was not possible for him to accomplish very much until he built-up this poor soil.

We are now considering the solution to this most important problem. The first phase of this is soil erosion. Soil erosion is simply the process whereby the surface of the earth together with all of its intermediate forms are sculptured and worn down.

Rainfall, sunshine, frost, wind, and the chemical action of the atmosphere combined to disintegrate and break down the rocks.

Surface waters, supplied by rain and melting snow or ice, wash down the particles of disintegrated rock into the valleys. Thence these fine materials are carried downward by streams and deposited along their channels or finally borne to the sea.

The tendency of erosion is to bring down the continents to a lowland or base plane a little above sea level. In another chapter Dr. Carver's methods are given on building up fertile soil.

Soil erosion is one of the most serious difficulties with which a great many farmers have to contend. For this reason I should think that whatever is said on the subject here is well worth the time.

Dr. Carver is still working on the soils at Tuskegee, to improve their composition of humus for plant food.

In any hilly country one can find banks of streams or ditches which show that from one to two or even more feet of soil have been washed down from adjacent hillsides and deposited on top of the soil originally at the surface. This original surface can be recognized by its black color.

Dr. Carver shows how the evil effects of erosion on fertility arises, in a large part, from the removal of the vegetable matter and of the finer silt and clay of the mineral portion of the soil. The great importance of vegetable matter in the soil, and how it can be readily removed by erosion is obvious. The silt and clay contains very much larger percentage of the essential elements for the plant growth than does the sandy portion. For this reason, the removal of the silt and clay, which of course are carried away because they can be held in suspension by the water, while the sand cannot, removes the most fertile part of the soil.

The proper management of these soils, and the successful growing of various crops, is the result of constant study and tireless efforts of Dr. Carver, through several years. In no better way could his creative ability be manifested than by this marvelous achievement.

In Dr. Moton's lecture to the Farmers' Conference, December 6, 1928, he said, "Thirty-eight years ago when Booker T. Washington called the first meeting of the Farmers' Conference there was widespread dissatisfaction in the South with the Negro farmer. Many of you here today recall what was being said. They said the negro was lazy, shiftless; that he wouldn't work unless he was made to; that he farmed extravagantly, pauperizing the soil; that he had no knowledge or capacity for agricultural economy; that he was a burden rather than an asset to the South.

"To those who made these charges they must have seemed true. They could point to example after example of Negro farmers who were shiftless, who never seemed to get ahead, and whose methods were wasteful. In the surface of it there may have been much to justify these charges. But Booker T. Washington, with that keen and understanding insight which characterized his life, saw beneath and beyond the surface. He too saw black farmers, housed in hovels, letting the soil go down and down, and failing to get the greatest production."

A group of members of the Carver School Farm Club, snapped as they paused a few minutes, while working on the Carver School Farm, Young, Miss.; (Route 1, Lumberton) Saturday, July 14, 1920.

A group of members of the Carver School Farm Club, snapped as they paused a few minutes, while working on the Carver School Farm, Young, Miss.; (Route 1, Lumberton) Saturday, July 14, 1920.

# CHAPTER VIII.

## THE CARVER SCHOOL FARM CLUB

In the agricultural section of South Mississippi, at a little place known as Young, (five miles east of Lumberton, the post office) a group of farmers organized the Carver School Farm Club, February 18, 1918.

It was the purpose of this organization to call the citizens of the community together in conference, from time to time; to discuss their industrial, moral and educational conditions; to exchange views; to present facts, and also to devise plans to do constructive work for the welfare of the community.

This organization was also composed of an inter-racial committee, which endeavored to study race relations from every point of view. Some of the leading white citizens took an active part in co-operating with this movement in bringing about a better understanding between the two races in that section.

During the first three years a school farm of four acres were maintained and cultivated by members of the Club. The money realized from sales of the crops was placed into the School Farm Treasury. This money was to be used in supplementing the length of the school term, and also in erecting a better school building and beautifying the school grounds.

## FROM A COMMERCIAL POINT OF VIEW.

"Is it a fact that Dr. Carver's various extractions from the peanut, the sweet potato and other products are being manufactured and put on the market?" one asked.

At present not a great deal has been done to utilize Dr. Carver's discoveries commercially. He says that he is merely scratching the surface of scientific investigations of the possibilities of the peanut and other Southern products.

There is no doubt, however, about the real commercial value of his products. He has one or more products on the market, sold by druggists, and it is said they are meritorious.

For an instance, there is Penol which is a medicine extracted from the peanut by the Carver Penol Company. Penol is recommended to be an excellent medicine for colds and other ailments. There is milk which Dr. Carver gets from the peanut, which is as good or better than cow's milk, Axle grease, ink etc., more than two hundred things altogether, a partial list of which is given in another chapter.

A prominent educator said, "It may be that Dr. Carver is far ahead of his time in attempting to develop supplementary uses from various Southern products."

The various recipes which are given in the supplementary section of this book, have no bearing whatever on the various products which Dr. Carver extracts from the peanut and the sweet potato. The recipes are simply from a household point of view on various ways of preparing the peanut, the sweet potato and other things for the table.

I make no attempt to give or make an appraisal of Dr. Carver's products. The future commercial possibilities of his products cannot be estimated.

In his scientific investigations Dr. Carver is blazing the way for young men and women who have the initiative of venturing into new fields of endeavor.

## SUNDAY EVENING BIBLE CLASS

One of Dr. Carver's side lines is that of his Sunday evening Bible class. This class has always been largely attended. It is very interesting for one to note how Dr. Carver conducts this class. As Mr. Jay S. Stowell says: "His teaching is of a unique sort. He illustrates stories of the Bible out of his own experience either as a boy or out of his laboratory work.

"The plague of locusts is to him just like the clouds of grasshoppers he used to see in Kansas as a boy. He insists that the spies knew that the promised Land was 'flowing with milk and honey' because they saw everywhere the long grass, and God never makes a grass country without putting cattle into it. They also knew about the honey because they found grapes, and without the bee to carry pollen to fertilize the grape blossoms the vine could not produce the marvelous bunches of fruit they found."

In order that his students may grasp the essential facts, he usually makes an illustration of everyday problems which are analogous with the subject which he may be discussing. Everyone takes an active part in the class, either by reading or in asking questions.

Dr. Carver has always been deeply religious beneath the surface. He believes in making right living the natural thing.

## HONORS.

As a result of Dr. Carver's visit to Oklahoma State Fair October 4-7, 1927, the colored junior high school at Tulsa, has been named after him.

I am informed that the building is just being completed, the cost of which amounted to several thousand dollars.

## (WHO'S WHO IN AMERICA)

At the 14th annual conference, 1923, of the National Association for the advancement of colored people he was granted the Spingard medal for his discoveries in agricultural chemistry. His work for the wider utilization of the sweet potato and the peanut, from which he has prepared 118 and 165 useful products respectively, formed the basis for the award, (Exp. Station Record, Vol. 49, p. 496, 1923).

Member of the Royal Society of Arts, London, 1917. His name was submitted without his knowledge of it.

# CHAPTER IX.

## STILL ACHIEVING AND HELPING PEOPLE

Dr. Carver is still actively engaged in carrying on his work. Apparently, he is as young, in spirit and action, as he was several years ago. That his optimistic and philosophical views of life have been prime factors in retaining his physical and mental strength, is obvious. It is probably due to this fact that he has been enabled to accomplish such remarkable results; and is still working for the betterment of his fellowmen.

He impresses one with admiration and reverence, with his unassuming and modest manner of living. He is a good-natured man, always in a cheerful and lively mood. Dr. Carver has always radiated this spirit of cheerfulness and good will wherever he has traveled in making lectures and demonstrations of his products.

Dr. Carver has not only been of service to the Southern Farmer in devising ways for greater production and marketing of his produce, but also in presenting the brighter side of life.

Obviously, he is doing a great work for the advancement of the agricultural industry, particularly in the Southern States.

He was a guest at the Negro State Fair at Oklahoma City, October 4-7, 1927. A full account of his visit is given by the Black Dispatch as follows:

## CARVER'S ADDRESS AT TULSA

(Used by permission of the Black Dispatch)

Tulsa, Oklahoma, October 11, 1927. Declaring that the wonderful scientific discoveries made by him in the field of botanical investigation were direct revelations of God, Dr. George Washington Carver, Tuskegee wizard and chemist of international fame, delivered an address here Friday night in

This beautiful silver cup, gold lined, 14 inches high and 6 inches across the top, bears the following inscription:
"Presented to Dr. Geo. W. Carver, by N. C. Negro Farmers Congress February 8, 1922, for distinguished Scientific Research."
This was given at the expiration of an eight days' tour through North Carolina, lecturing on the possibilities of the sweet potato. He had with him the 118 different products.

This beautiful silver cup, gold lined, 14 inches high and 6 inches across the top, bears the following inscription: "Presented to Dr. Geo. W. Carver, by N. C. Negro Farmers Congress February 8, 1922, for distinguished Scientific Research."

This was given at the expiration of an eight days' tour through North Carolina, lecturing on the possibilities of the sweet potato. He had with him the 118 different products.the rooms of the Security Life Insurance Company. Carver was a guest of the Negro State Fair officials. His collection of more than 90 products from the peanut were on display all week at the Fair Grounds.

## RELIGIOUS INCLINATIONS

Dr. Carver in his discourse, disclosed deep religious inclinations as indicated by his constant use of the scriptures to drive home a shaft of truth, his favorite expressions during the discourse being, " 'Study to show thyself approved of God' "Ye shall know the truth and the truth shall set you free', 'Behold, look, I have given you every herb, to you it shall be meat.' "

## PEOPLE PERISH

" 'Where there is no vision the people perish' again resorting to the scriptures, Dr. Carver brought realism and actualities home to his audience when he pointed out that in the early morning hours he had treked up Sand Hill and had found 27 new plants indigenous to the soil of Oklahoma containing medicinal properties.' 'I found down in Ferguson's Drug Store on North Greenwood,' continued Carver 'seven patent medicines containing in their formulas certain elements contained in these plants on Sand Pipe Hill. The preparations were shipped in from New York, they should be shipped in from Sand Pipe Hill[.]' Dr. Carver clinched his scripture grip on his audience by the laconic expression, 'My people are perishing for the lack of knowledge.' "

## OIL IS HERE

Referring to the oil industry and the difficulties that block and obstruct its production, and at the same time pointing to opportunities open to the fertile brain of some geological wizard of the future, Dr. Carver said, "Some day, somewhere, some man is going to say 'Oil is here and oil is there,' and oil will be where he lays his fingers. The whole theory of geological science is going to be revolutionized; it might just as well be some member of this audience who will do this as anyone else. Such a discovery will mark the end of 'dry holes' in the search for liquid gold, and that day is coming," continued the speaker.

## VENEER ISN'T WORTH ANYTHING

Standing there bent with age, the noted speaker and chemist frowned down upon the class of folk who seek truth in shallow places. "Life requires thorough preparation. Veneer isn't worth anything: we must disabuse our people of the idea that there is a short cut to achievement, we must understand that education after all is nothing more than seeking and understanding relations of one thing to another. First you get an idea about a given thing, then you attempt to drift back to the cause, there is a life study in the attempt to determine first causes in any given thing."

## SWEET POTATO IS MORNING GLORY

As an illustration of what he meant Dr. Carver went on to point out that in the study of the sweet potato one must first understand that the sweet potato was not a potato at all, but belonged to the morning glory family. "If you did not know this in the outset, every step you made would be in the wrong direction," he continued.

## MUST STUDY

"Science is truth, a theory is a theory only because it lacks truth. The Bible gives us the best support in this conception when we read, 'We shall know the truth and the truth shall set you free,' and then it says again in support of application and concentration, 'Study to show thyself approved of God.' Is it not meet and proper that we should make our contribution to civilization?"

## DOES THE NEGRO IMITATE?

"The world is looking for creative minds, creative genius is what makes people respect you. It's not a color question, it's a question of whether you have what the world wants. We can conquer if we will only do it. In this connection the speaker said that following one of his lectures and demonstrations in a Southern city, a white Southerner arose in the audience to make a confession. He said to his white friends, "I was taught by my father that a colored man never thought independently. He told me that a white child and a Negro child were the same up to their 12th year, after then the white child began to advance, while the Negro began to imitate. I want to ask my white friends tonight, who has this Negro imitated." "He sat down without another word," continued Carver, "and nobody answered his question."

## GOD, WHAT IS A PEANUT?

"Why if one knows the peanut, he can find food and shelter, he can produce medicine out of that same peanut, washing powders also come, face bleach, candy, boards used in the wall of a home. God, what is a peanut, and why did you make it?" exclaimed Carver in one of his dramatic climaxes. The fact that Carver has found more than 90 different things that can be located wholly or in part out of the peanut shows that he knows what he was talking about when he said, "Ye shall know science and science shall make you free."

The Carver exhibit at the Fair contained the following:

Soap and soap sticks, a dozen or more beverages with peanut basis, mixed pickles, milk, milk curds, sauce, sprouted peanuts, many forms of candy, meal, instant and dry coffee, oils, ink, breakfast food, stock food, salve, bleach, tan remover, many specimens of wood filler and paint adjuncts, remedies for many things, washing powder, and a variety of combinations of peanut shells and peanut skins with waste paper made into insulating boards.

## HIGH POINTS--CARVER CARVES

"Creative genius is what make people respect you. It's not a color question, it's a question of whether you have what the world wants."

"You never saw a heavy thinker with his mouth open--Stop talking so much."

"The first thing one must learn about a sweet potato is that it is a morning glory."

"Education is seeking relations."

"You can't teach people anything, you can only draw out."

"When you find a teacher who does all the talking in the class room, take your child away from her."

"A theory is a theory because it lacks truth."

"We must disabuse our people of the idea that there is a short cut to achievement."

"Life requires thorough preparation; veneer isn't worth anything."

"The whole structure of scientific thought is going to be revolutionized."

"Anything that helps fill a dinner pail is valuable."

"Where there is no vision there is no hope."

"Is it not meet and proper that we as a race should make our contribution to civilization?"

"Ye shall know science and science shall make you free."

"As I look at the giddy young people in Tulsa jazzing around on the streets, my thought is, 'How much can the world depend on you?'"

"A group of white men here say they want a man who can locate oil more accurately. They forgot to say whether they wanted a white man, a red man, a yellow or black man; they only said they wanted a man who could locate oil."

"When you can do the common things of life in an uncommon way, you will command attention of the world."

Recently after returning from the State Fair which was held in Oklahoma City, Dr. Carver received an invitation to speak and make a display of his products at Columbia University, New York City. As a rule he accepts as many invitations as he can get to without interfering too much with his regular line of duties at Tuskegee. He was not able, however, to accept this invitation to speak at Columbia. There is scarcely a day passes but what Dr. Carver does not receive a letter requesting him to speak at some place in the country. It isn't possible for him to accept all invitations which are constantly being extended to him.

During last spring Dr. Carver made a very extensive tour through Tennessee and Virginia. A full account of which is given by the Tuskegee messenger and the Highland Echo, Maryville College, Tennessee. He has received letters from people asking him to return to make another series of lectures.

After this tour Dr. Carver was invited to his Alma Mater, Simpson College, Indianola, Iowa, June 1928, where an honorary degree of Doctor of Science was conferred upon him.

## Professor Carver Ends College Tour*

Professor George Carver, famous agricultural chemist of Tuskegee Institute and fellow of the Royal Society of London, has recently completed a remarkable tour among the colleges of Virginia and Tennessee, under the auspices of the interracial Commission and the student department of the Y. M. C. A. Taking along an elaborate exhibit of his remarkable peanut products. Prof. Carver addressed large audiences at Ashland, Randolph-Macon, Bridgewater College, Lynchburg College, Harrison State Teachers' College, Virginia polytechnic, St. Paul's Normal, Washington and Lee, the Virginia Prep School Conference, Tusculum and Maryville Colleges and other institutions.

At Maryville, Professor Carver spoke for an hour to an audience of more than five hundred. At Virginia Prep School he was heard by perhaps the largest audience ever assembled in the Y. M. C. A. auditorium. At the end of an hour the chairman announced that the meeting was adjourned, but nobody moved. The audience remained forty-five minutes longer to ask questions, and even then many of the students were unwilling to go. In the evening Professor Carver spoke at the B. Y. P. U. meeting, and next morning, an invitation of the chemistry professors, gave a lecture to all the chemistry classes. At Teachers' College, Harrisonburg, he was heard by three hundred and fifty young women who are preparing to teach. These experiences are illustrative of the extraordinary impression Dr. Carver made wherever he went. The newspapers everywhere were most generous in their comments. Many of the institutions are asking that Professor Carver be sent back for another series.

The tour was arranged by Mr. Forest D. Brown, State Student Secretary of the Y. M. C. A., who accompanied Professor Carver and looked after his comfort.

# THE TUSKEGEE MESSENGER,

# June 30, 1928.

(* Used by permission of The Tuskegee Messenger).

## NOTED NEGRO SCIENTIST SPEAKS TO STUDENTS.

## Dr. Geo. W. Carver, of Tuskegee, Gives Talk on "Inside of a Peanut."

To some it is given, at least once in a lifetime to stand in the presence of greatness.

Those five or six hundred students who heard Dr. George W. Carver, Negro scientist of Tuskegee Institute, who spoke to us on last Tuesday afternoon, are confident that they sat under the voice of one deservedly called great. If one may judge from their interest and overwhelming enthusiasm, he is confident also that these students were aware of the greatness of their opportunity and were humble.

As a personality, Dr. Carver proved to be more than we who had been reading his biographies had anticipated; as a speaker, he charmed us with his directness and delightful whimsicalities; as a creative scientist, he so astounds us that one forgets whatever praise-sounding words he once had known, but they would not have been adequate anyway. One says, Here is a man who has really caught the spirit of Science. Another says, Here is a man of God! And both are right, for, as Dr. Carver himself would say, Science is Truth, and all Truth is of God.

For us the humble peanut has become glorified, for out of it we now know that one man has taken the materials for compounding two hundred and two useful products, he himself giving us the assurance that its possibilities are not yet exhausted. What with peanut milk, buttermilk and cream, cheese and coffee, relish and sauces, coffee and peanut sprouts, cooking fat and mock oysters, one is tempted to say that we might have a balanced diet of peanut products alone. Add to these paper made from peanut shells, artificial silk from the same source, other peanut products such as soap stock, ink, tooth paste, dandruff cure, wood stains, dyes, beauty creams and lotions, pharmaceutical preparations as: emulsions for goiters and creosote that are stable and satisfactory, etc., and one is tempted to say that we could lead a normal comfortable life using only peanut products to meet our daily needs.

Dr. Carver had time to only hint at the work he has done with pecans and potatoes. He has succeeded in producing one thousand dyes from vegetable substances, including forty-nine from the scuppernong grape alone. His work in producing beautiful, lasting colors from the clay of Georgia and Alabama sounds like a miracle and whether his talk of sextuple oxidation, a reaction not recognized by chemistry was more mystifying to the scientific or the non-scientific listener is a question that remains to be settled.

We know that, though he talked to us for an hour and let us crowd about him while he packed his bottled specimens, we glimpsed at only the fringe of his vast knowledge. But at least we may sense a new something of the infinite possibilities tied up in ordinary everyday things. More important than that is the new vision of Man's unlimited capacity for a growing understanding of the mind of the Maker, and, as a consequence of that a new reverence for this being we call Man.

# THE HIGHLAND ECHO,

## Maryville, Tennessee, April 27, 1928.

(Reproduced by permission of Mr. Robert T. Dance, Maryville College, Tenn.)

While questioning him about his discoveries, he told me that he was only blazing a path, and that he had only scratched the surface. He avers that the possibilities of the peanut and the sweet potato have not been exhausted by any means. In diverting any praise which comes to him, he ascribes the results of his work as being direct revelations from God. "To Him all credit should be given," said Dr. Carver.

As usual, he took an active part in the Alabama State Fair, last fall, which was held at Montgomery. For several years he has maintained a booth at The State Fair at Montgomery, where his products have been on display. In another chapter in a letter from Mr. Grover C. Hall, Editor of the Montgomery Advertiser. He says, "Dr. Carver's products are viewed with interest by people from all over the state and that he is much esteemed in Alabama."

The Negro Farmers' Conference held its annual meeting at Tuskegee Institute, recently after the State Fair ended. The Conference opened the 6th of this month, December. After returning from the State Fair Dr. Carver prepared for the Conference, in which he has always taken a very active part.

When this great wizard chemist shall have returned to his resting place, I venture the prediction, that his name will be graven in the walls among the immortals in the American Hall of Fame, as a revealer of the possibilities of the peanut, the sweet potato, a great scientist, a great painter, a great advocate for the advancement of the agricultural industry and of new foods, and as a great American and brother to all mankind.

Dr. Carver has not been affected by all the praise and honor conferred upon him. With his quiet, unassuming and pleasing manner, he goes about his duties as usual, conscientious of doing the will of the Great Nazerene, and rendering service for the betterment of his fellowmen.

# CHAPTER X.

## VIEWS AND COMMENTS

This chapter is devoted to views and comments from business and professional people on Dr. Carver's work.

### THE ATLANTA CONSTITUTION

(Atlanta, Georgia, August 27, 1928).

I have watched the result of Dr. Carver's investigation with intense interest and you probably recall that we carried a long article in the Constitution some months ago about his work.

He has rendered a wonderful service not only to the South but to the whole country and his genius has made him a national character in the field of science.

He should receive every possible encouragement in his further efforts.

Very truly yours,

Clark Howell, Editor


### THE MONTGOMERY ADVERTISER

(Montgomery, Alabama, August 27, 1928).

I greatly admire Dr. Carver and know about his work in a general way. Some of it I have seen; but I am not sufficiently familiar with it to attempt a serious appraisal of its merit. He has one or more commercial products on the market, sold by druggists, and I am told they are meritorious. He has done some important research work on the peanut in particular, but this does not mark the limit of his endeavors. He is a zealous laboratory worker, honestly scientific in spirit, and is much esteemed in Alabama. He has a booth at the State Fair every Fall and his work is viewed with interest by people from all over the State.

                                      Grover C. Hall, Editor The Advertiser.

## ALABAMA POLYTECHNIC INSTITUTE

                         (Auburn, Alabama, August 18, 1928).

Dr. Carver has already impressed me as being imbued with an earnest spirit of service and an intense desire to forward the best interests of the agricultural industry. I am sure Dr. Carver has attacked some very interesting and significant problems relative to the complete utilization of our Southern products. It may be that he is far ahead of his time in attempting to develop supplementary uses for various products.

Dr. Carver has always impressed me as consecrating himself to doing something for his fellowmen rather than profiting commercially by the results of his labors.

Very truly yours,

                                J. D. Pope, Agricultural Economist.

## THE PHILADELPHIA TRIBUNE

                         (Philadelphia, Pa., August 14, 1928).

Dr. Carver's achievements in his chosen field undoubtedly places him in the front rank of present-day scientists, and make him a man whom the Negro may justly be proud.

Very truly yours,

E. Washington Rhodes, Editor The Philadelphia Tribune.

## ATLANTA UNIVERSITY

(Atlanta, Georgia, August 24, 1928).

I have known Dr. Geo. W. Carver for a number of years, and have watched his work with great interest. His diligence, his personality and his unusual skill have commanded general respect in all quarters.

Not being an expert in such matters, I am naturally unfamiliar with the commercial value of his discoveries. But they are of interest, worthy of admiration, and some of them, it would surely seem, will prove of real commercial value.

M. W. Adams, President.

## TOUGALOO COLLEGE

Tougaloo, Mississippi, September 4, 1928).

Prof. Geo. W. Carver, of Tuskegee Institute, has lectured many times at Tougaloo College during the past fifteen years of my presidency, and I am greatly impressed with the value of his work as a pioneer in scientific investigation. It is pioneering both in the sense that Prof. Carver has discovered values hitherto unrealized in common Southern products such as the peanut, the sweet potato, and various clays, and in the sense that he is the first Negro scientist to have achieved this kind of success.

Sincerely yours,

William T. Holmes, President.

## FISK UNIVERSITY

(Nashville, Tenn., Sept. 11, 1928).

I have met Dr. Carver and have gone through his laboratory at Tuskegee. The work that he has done appears to be remarkable both in quality and variety. But the personality of the man is probably as impressive as his work. Quiet and unassuming with a mystical approach to God he inspires one with admiration and reverence.

Sincerely yours,

Thomas E. Jones, President.

## LINCOLN UNIVERSITY

(Chester County, Pa., Sept. 13, 1928).

By his achievements in the utilization of agricultural products Dr. George W. Carver, of Tuskegee Institute, has made himself an economic asset not only to the South but to the nation. He has found what the late Dr. Russell Conwell called "acres of diamonds" in things near at hand. His career should inspire alert and ambitious young men to find in the common objects and opportunities of life a field for useful and distinguished service.

Wm. Hallock Johnson, President of Lincoln University.

## NORTH CAROLINA COLLEGE FOR NEGROES

(Durham, North Carolina, Sept. 13, 1928).

Dr. George W. Carver is one of the great scientists of the world. He has taken the humble peanut and exalted it until today the things which can be produced from a peanut are multitudinous and marvelous.

Dr. Carver is a man of the greatest humility, a true seeker after knowledge and truth, is always humble. This to my mind is one of the truest tests of greatness.

Dr. Carver has demonstrated to the world that the Negro is capable of making new discoveries in the scientific field, that the Negro can blaze a path where before everything was a dense wilderness, he has caused light to shine in dark places, therefore, he has added much to the prestige of the race. The whole race is grateful and appreciative of the labors of this wonderful man and scientist. I sincerely hope that he will be spared for many years to do research work along scientific lines.

I am honored in being permitted to utter these words of appreciation for a man who needs no recommendation at the hands of anyone. His labors and successes speak for themselves.

Respectfully yours,

James E. Shepard, President.

## HAMPTON INSTITUTE

(Hampton, Va., Sept. 14, 1928).

I have known Dr. Carver for more than ten years and have been impressed, as anyone is who knows him, by his scientific learning, his originality, and the breadth and nobility of his philosophical and religious outlook upon life.

Though not a great deal has been done as yet, apparently, to utilize his discoveries commercially, I should suppose that they must eventually be of decided value in the production of peanuts and sweet potatoes and other crops of the South.

Sincerely yours,

James E. Gregg, Principal.

## STRAIT COLLEGE

(New Orleans, La., Sept. 14, 1928).

I met Dr. Carver at a Farmer's Conference in Baton Rouge, and visited his laboratory at Tuskegee one day during his absence.

My impression, however, has been that he was a man of very high character and outstanding ability, and that he has done a very valuable and very successful piece of work. I have felt that the doctor and his accomplishments were of high value to the world at large and in particular to Tuskegee Institute and the Negro race.

Cordially yours,

James P. O'Brien, President.

## VIRGINIA UNION UNIVERSITY

(Richmond, Virginia, Sept. 18, 1928).

I consider Dr. Carver one of the most progressive and successful citizens of the present day. His accomplishments are almost beyond belief.

Very truly yours,

Wm. John Clark, President.

## SELMA UNIVERSITY

(Selma, Alabama, Sept. 18, 1928).

I regard Dr. Carver as being a remarkable character making a great contribution to the economic life of the Negro race, and to our whole country. It is hardly conceivable that Dr. Carver has gotten out more than three hundred products from the peanut and sweet potato.

I am very glad to learn that you are planning to put in book form Dr. Carver's wonderful achievement.

Yours truly,

R. T. Pollard, President.

## MEHARRY MEDICAL COLLEGE

(Nashville, Tenn., Sept. 17, 1928).

I have had an acquaintance with Dr. Carver for several years. I consider him one of the most ingenuous of modern chemists, in fact, it is almost weird to see this beautiful sweet natured gentleman extract almost innumerable products and by-products from the lowly peanut and the sweet potato and the common clays of the Southland.

Dr. Carver has done a wonderful work in Chemistry that has brought honor and will bring still greater honor to himself, Tuskegee Institute, and to the race of men.

With best wishes for your work, I am, fraternally yours,

John J. Mullowney, Pres.

## HOWARD UNIVERSITY

(Washington, D. C., Sept. 19, 1928).

I feel wholly disqualified to pass a judgment of any critical value on Professor Carver's remarkable discoveries, as his sphere of work falls in specific scientific fields with which my knowledge is entirely general. I am, therefore, content to join the ranks of his admirers and wonder at the marvelous things which he has wrought. His work has brought great credit to the Negro race.

Yours truly,

Kelly Miller.

## SHAW UNIVERSITY

(Raleigh, N. C., Sept. 22, 1928).

I cannot commend too highly the work of our mutual friend, Dr. George W. Carver. I regard him as one of the greatest scientists of the age. It is simply beyond all comprehension what he has been able to accomplish in the field of chemistry. It fills one with admiration to visit his laboratory, and to observe the many products of his skillful research.

The beauty of this man's life is that he does not desire publicity but carries on in the most modest fashion, giving God all the glory for what has been accomplished. It is refreshing in these days to find a man so thoroughly scientific and at the same time so spiritual.

He told me at one time that he had merely scratched the surface of scientific investigation. I trust he may live many years to get below the surface and to give to the world many more manifestations of his wonderful skill.

Very sincerely yours,

Joseph L. Peacock, President.

518 Fourth Avenue, Pittsburgh, Pa.
August 30, 1928.

I do not feel capable of criticizing a man of Dr. Carver's talent.

Candidly, I visited Tuskegee and went through his chemical laboratory and it was just as clear to me as mud, because I simply listened as all others do with my mouth and ears open, and at the finish I really didn't know how it was all done. I asked him one question and his answer confused me. The question I asked him was this: "Dr. Carver, you have here hundreds of results which may be called discoveries, and you have made all of these discoveries in this laboratory,--have you anywhere written formulas for each and every one of these discoveries you have made?" I asked him this question because I thought of what might happen in case of his death. If he had the formulas for all of his discoveries, then his work would not be lost to science, but if he did not have formulas for what he has done, but is simply carrying them around in his head, you can see how futile all of his work will be when he finally passes on. To my amazement, Dr. Carver looked at me and smiled and said, "I have all of these formulas, but I have not written them down yet"; and I told him that I thought he was doing himself and the race as well as science a great injustice not to have each and every formula down in a book somewhere to be left at Tuskegee as evidence of his scientific knowledge.

Yours very truly,

Robert L. Vann, Attorney at Law.

## THE CHEYNEY TRAINING SCHOOL FOR TEACHERS

(Cheyney, Pennsylvania, Sept. 28, 1928).

I had the privilege of knowing Dr. Carver directly at Tuskegee for about three years, but I can claim no very special knowledge of his work beyond what is generally known to the public. Dr. Carver is not only a scientist and creative genius in the various projects to which you refer, but he is an artist whose remarkable work in the painting of flowers is all too little known. His art exhibits at Tuskegee used to be, and I hope still continue to be, notable occasions. A man of truly unique personality and wholly unselfish in his great sercives, he made a lasting impression on all who knew him.

I have only one serious apprehension with regard to Dr. Carver. That is, that as far as I know he has left no written account of his researches and discoveries. This means that his work is likely to pass with him. That will be a very great loss to the race.

Wishing you the fullest measure of success in your generous undertaking, I am,

Sincerely yours,

Leslie Pickney Hill, Principal.

## TALLADEGA COLLEGE

(Talladega, Alabama, Sept. 25, 1928).

I am very glad to express my high appreciation of the character and worth of Dr. Carver personally and of the untold value that his scientific investigations have for the development of the agricultural industry. There is no doubt about the real worth of his investigations and the value of the work for the future cannot well be estimated.

Very sincerely yours,

F. A. Sumner, President.

## TUSKEGEE INSTITUTE

(Tuskegee, Alabama, Sept. 26, 1928).

Years ago Dr. Washington was attracted to Professor Carver by his thorough scientific knowledge in agriculture, chemistry and botany, and asked him to come to Tuskegee where he has remained ever since, at different times in charge of our Agricultural

Department, our Experiment Station and latterly devoting his entire time to research work in the laboratory.

Dr. Carver has made some remarkable discoveries in food products and in the utilization of the by-products of industry, particularly has he given a new value to the peanut, the sweet potato, the soy bean and the common clays.

He is a scholar in the real sense of the word. His knowledge is extensive and accurate, while in his personality he remains simple and modest. He has the humility of true greatness, and not the least of his services, has been his work in affecting better inter-racial understanding and good will through his lectures and demonstrations before students of white schools and colleges, both North and South.

R. R. Moton, Principal.

## SOUTHERN UNIVERSITY

(Baton Rouge, La., Sept. 26, 1928).

Dr. Carver has made a great contribution to the Negro race, and to the people of America in general. It has been my good fortune to come in contact with Dr. Carver many times. He has been invited to lecture to the students of Southern University on several occasions, as well as to address our Farmers' Conferences, and each time he has exhibited some of the products he produced under scientific treatment. I consider him a genius. In my opinion, only a few men who are scientists in America can be placed in his class.

In addition to Dr. Carver's technical training, he is a conscientious student, and satisfied himself with results only. As an outstanding evidence of his ability, the sweet potato and the peanut have given new values and higher potentialities of their worth than ever before.

Dr. Carver's lectures are instructive and interesting throughout, and his demonstrations are of his work, and not of himself. He has given the world new values of Agricultural products, and he will go down in history as being one of the greatest scientists of the age. He is a man, not only of ability, but of firm character in the principles of right and fair dealings. Dr. Carver is not only a lecturer and a teacher, but he is an original producer, and a profound thinker.

With best wishes for the success of your good work, I am,

Yours very truly,

J. S. Clark, President.


## FLORIDA NORMAL AND COLLEGIATE INSTITUTE

(St. Augustine, Fla., September 29, 1928).

I regard Dr. Carver as the foremost man of our group in America in his particular line.

N. W. Collier, President.


## UNITED STATES DEPARTMENT OF AGRICULTURE

(Washington, D. C., October 30, 1928).

I believe that Dr. Carver's work speaks for itself and that any comment which I might make would be superfluous. He has undoubtedly done a great deal to popularize the use of both peanuts and sweet potatoes, and must be looked upon as one of the leading investigators along these lines.

Very truly yours,

                        J. H. Beattie, Associate Horticulturist.

## STORER COLLEGE

                        Harper's Ferry, W. Va., Dec. 5, 1928).

Dr. Carver is the most distinguished chemist produced by the Negro race in America. Among men of science his achievements are so well known that to enumerate them is to add no praise to the accomplishments of a great modest man.

In his contributions to scientific knowledge he belongs to no race, any more than the facts of science which he has adduced may be classified by any formula of pigmentation.

In his unaffected simplicity he is an inspiration, his scientific achievements command our admiration and his works make him a brother to all mankind.

                        Henry T. McDonald, President.

## UNIVERSITY OF GEORGIA

                        Office of the Chancellor
                        (Athens, Georgia, December 17, 1928).

I have heard a great deal about Doctor Carver's work. The reports I have read indicate that he is doing a real service in advancing the economic interests of the South.

                        Chas. M. Smelling.

## NORTH CAROLINA MUTUAL LIFE INSURANCE COMPANY

(Durham, North Carolina, December 14, 1928).

Dr. Carver has convincingly demonstrated the possibilities of getting food products from commodities that heretofore seemed almost worthless and is rendering distinctive service in this field. He deserves the commendation and appreciation of all American people.

C. C. Spaulding, President.


## OLD CHERRY STREET BAPTIST CHURCH

Organized in 1809
16th Christian Streets,
(Philadelphia, Pa., December 19, 1928).

It is a pleasure to note that Dr. George W. Carver, of Tuskegee, Alabama, is one of the greatest chemists of the age. He is a practical chemist with that rare gift, a scientific imagination. He is one of the distinguished scientists of the age. He proves to the world that the Negro has an original ability as well as men of other races. There is no one in our race of which we are more proud than Dr. George W. Carver.

Dr. Carver has made nature disclose many of its great secrets as probably no other chemist has done. He reflects credit upon his great Creator as few chemists do, through that wonderful scientific mind, he has certainly discovered many of the Great Maker's wonders--in the peanut, sweet potato, pecan and clay. He is a wonderful inspiration for all young life, and especially those scientifically inclined.

He is deeply religious and credits his ability to the God whom he faithfully serves. Any time spent in his presence discloses that you are in touch with a wonderful master mind and an illustrious soul.

W. A. Harrod, Pastor.

## UNITED STATES DEPARTMENT OF AGRICULTURE

Bureau of Chemistry and Soils<br>(Washington, D. C., December 20, 1928).

I have looked up Dr. Carver's record which we have on file, a copy of which I am enclosing herewith. Unfortunately I do not know Dr. Carver personally, but inquiries in the Department indicate that it is felt that he has accomplished considerable for the Negro race in America.

Henry G. Knight, Chief of Bureau.

## SIMPSON COLLEGE

(Washington, D. C., December 20, 1928).

Dr. Carver's career has been an inspiration to very many young people. When I consider the difficulty with which he had to contend, I am amazed at what he has accomplished. His spirit and character are even more wonderful than his accomplishments.

He was a student at Simpson College for three years. He took his degree in Agriculture at State College at Ames, and gave such promise that he was retained for some time in the faculty there until he was called to Tuskegee Institute.

Our College conferred upon him the honorary degree of Doctor of Science last commencement.

John L. Hillman, President.

## IOWA STATE COLLEGE

(Ames, Iowa, December 18, 1928).

It has not been my privilege to know Mr. George W. Carver, of Tuskegee Institute, but from inquiry of his many friends and former instructors, who are still connected with Iowa State College, I learn that his great asset is persistency.

He came to this college in the fall of 1890 and was graduated in the class of 1894. He had at that time a great love and desire for scientific training. He received his greatest inspiration in the line of science from Dr. Louis H. Pammel of the Botany Department, and from that inspiration he became a strong scientific investigator. As a college we are more than pleased with the great work which he has been doing, and we extend to him our congratulations and wish for him many years in his chosen line of work.

Sincerely yours,

R. M. Hughes, President.

# SUPPLEMENT

## CHAPTER XI.

## 105 DIFFERENT WAYS TO PREPARE THE PEANUT FOR THE TABLE
## SUPPLEMENT

This section is composed entirely of Dr. Carver's bulletins, in which much of his work is recorded. Very helpful information is to be found here which should be of interest to all people in all walks of life. It deals with the production of food and various ways of preparing it. Wholesome foods prepared properly is of universal importance to everybody. Hence, everyone should find this section not only interesting, but instructive as well.

When Dr. Carver was questioned about the products which he extracted from the peanut he said, "The milk may be condensed or dried the same as cow's milk. Butter can be made from the milk, but it is easier and more satisfactorily made from the oils and fat direct.

"The sweet mil, when used in making yeast bread, gives a loaf or rolls of exceedingly rich flavor, very similar to the prized milk bread.

"The rich cream may be used on fruits, in coffee, on breakfast cereals, and makes the most acceptable substitute for the cream from cow's milk, that is known.

"The whey, which is a very pretty pale straw color, makes a delicious beverage when iced and flavored to taste. It has few, if any, superior products for making fancy fruit punches."

The official bulletin on the peanut is as follows:

Of all the money crops grown, perhaps there are none more promising than the peanut in its several varieties and their almost limitless possibilities.

Of the good things in their favor, the following stand out as most promising:

1. Like all other members of the pod-bearing family, they enrich the soil.

2. They are easily and cheaply grown.

3. For man the nuts possess a wider range of food value than any other legume.

4. The nutritive value of the hay as a stock food compares favorably with that of the cow pea.

5. They are easy to plant, easy to grow and easy to harvest.

6. The great food-and-forage value of the peanut will increase in proportion to the rapidity with which we make it a real study. This will increase consumption, and therefore, must increase production.

7. In this county two crops per year of the Spanish variety can be raised.

8. The peanut exerts a dietetic or a medicinal effect upon the human system that is very desirable.

9. I doubt if there is another foodstuff that can so universally be eaten, in some form, by every individual.

10. Pork fattened from peanuts and hardened off with a little corn just before killing, is almost if not quite equal to the famous Red-gravy hams or the world renowned Beechnut breakfast bacon.

11. The nuts yield a high percentage of oil of superior quality.

12. The clean cake, after the oil has been removed, is very high in muscle-building properties (protein), and the ease with which the meal blends in with flour, meal, etc., makes it of especial value to bakers, confectioners, candy-makers, and ice cream factories.

13. Peanut oil is one of the best known vegetable oils.

14. A pound of peanuts contains a little more of the body-building nutrients than a pound of sirloin steak, while of the heat energy-producing nutrients it has more than twice as much.

## VARIETIES

There are many varieties of the peanut, all possessing more or less merit. A number have been tested here on our Station grounds and we can heartily recommend the following varieties in the order named:

1st. The Spanish. As compared with most other varieties the vines are small, upright in growth, with nearly all the pods clinging close to the tap-root; hence, they can be planted closer together and the yield will be larger.

This variety produced 59 bushels per acre on very light, sandy soil.

2nd. The Georgia and Tennessee Red. These are practically one and the same variety--habit of growth and fruiting qualities are much the same as the Spanish--with us it made a lightly lower yield.

This variety had from three to four kernels to the pod. The nuts are rich in flavor.

3rd. The Virginia Running Variety. This variety is often referred to as the typical American peanut.

## AS FOOD FOR MAN

By reason of its superior food value the peanut has become almost a universal diet for man, and when we learn its real value, I think I am perfectly safe in the assertion that it will not only become a prime essential in every well balanced dietary, but a real necessity. Indeed, I do not know of any one vegetable that has such a wide range of food possibilities.

Below are given 105 ways of preparing the peanut for human consumption, I hope that every farmer will learn to appreciate them and raise large quantities for his own consumption; and also with the hope that the city folk will find the diet not only wholesome, satisfying, healthful and appetizing, but very economical. Fourteen recipes were selected from this number, and a five course luncheon served to ten food specialists; and each one without exception was enthusiastic over it, and said it was the most satisfying luncheon he or she had eaten.

### NO. 1, PEANUT SOUP

- 1 quart of milk,
- 2 tablespoonfuls butter,
- 2 tablespoonfuls flour,
- 1 cup peanuts.

Cook peanuts until soft; remove skins, mash or grind until very fine; let milk come to a boil; add the peanuts; cook 20 minutes.

Rub flour into a smooth paste with milk; add butter to the peanuts and milk; stir in flour; season with salt and pepper to taste. Serve hot.

### NO. 2, PEANUT SOUP NUMBER TWO

Take roasted peanuts; grind or mash real fine; to every half a pint add a quart of milk, half a teaspoon salt, one saltspoon pepper, one small onion minced very fine, one bay leaf, one stalk celery chopped very fine or a salt spoon celery seed. Cook for fifteen minutes. Great care must be exercised to keep from burning.

Moisten one tablespoon of corn starch in a quarter cup of cold milk; add to the soup; stir until thick and smooth; strain through a fine sieve, and serve with peanut wafers.

## NO. 3, PEANUT BISQUE

To 3 cups of boiling milk add half a teaspoon chopped onion, a pinch of salt and pepper; rub to a smooth paste a tablespoon of flour with water; add half cup of peanut butter; stir in the flour; boil 3 minutes longer; serve with peanut wafers.

## NO. 4, PEANUT SOUP NUMBER FOUR

Boil ten minutes in half a cup of water, half a cup of chopped celery, a tablespoon of chopped onion, the same amount of red and green peppers mixed; add a cup of peanut butter and three cups of rich milk to which has been added one tablespoon flour; add one teaspoon of sugar; boil two minutes and serve.

## NO. 5, CONSOMME OF PEANUTS

Take 1 pint of shelled peanuts; boil or steam until the skins can be removed; boil in salted water until nearly all the water boils away; add 1 quart of beef stock, a few grains of cayenne, half a teaspoon salt; let boil slowly for ten minutes; serve hot.

## NO. 6, PUREE OF PEANUTS

- 1 pint of peanuts blanched and ground,
- 1 pint milk,
- ½ cup cream,
- 1 tablespoon butter,

- 1 egg, well beaten.

Let the milk and cream come to a boil; stir in all the other ingredients; add more milk if too thick; salt and pepper to taste; serve at once with peanut wafers.

## NO. 7, PUREE OF PEANUTS NUMBER TWO

(Extra fine)

Take 1 pint of peanuts, roast until the shells rub off easily (do not brown); grind very fine; add a salt spoon of salt; 1 teaspoon sugar; pour on boiling water, and stir until thick as cream. Set in double boiler and boil from eight to ten hours; set away and allow to get thoroughly cold; turn out. Can be eaten hot or cold. When sliced, rolled in bread crumbs or cracker dust and fried a chicken brown, it makes an excellent substitute for meat. A generous layer between slices of bread makes an excellent sandwich.

## NO. 8, PEANUT BREAD ONE

Into any good biscuit dough work in a liberal supply of blanched and ground nuts; roll out thin; cut in small discs, and bake in a quick oven; serve hot.

## NO. 9, PEANUT BREAD NUMBER TWO

- ½ cupful sugar,
- 2 teaspoons baking powder,
- ½ cupful blanched and chopped nuts,
- ½ cupful sweet milk,
- 1 egg, beat in,
- 2 cup-fulls sifted flour.

Mix these ingredients; make into small loaves or biscuits; let rise for one-half hour; bake in slow oven until done, which will require about fifty minutes.

### NO. 10, ENGLISH PEANUT BREAD

- 2 cups liquid yeast,
- 1 tablespoon butter,
- 2 tablespoons sugar,
- 1 teaspoon of salt.

Stir flour with a spoon, beat it long and hard; let stand in a warm place until light; bake in a moderate oven one hour; blanched and finely-chopped peanuts; add flour to make a soft dough; let stand in a warm place until light; bake in a moderate oven one hour.

### NO. 11, AUNT NELLIE'S PEANUT BROWN BREAD

- 1½ cups white flour,
- 1½ cups Graham flour,
- 2 teaspoons baking powder,
- ½ cup sweet milk, or just enough to make a soft dough,
- 1 teaspoon salt,
- ½ cup blanched and ground peanuts.

"Mix well together and bake in a moderate oven.

### NO. 12, OAT MEAL PEANUT BREAD (DELICIOUS)

- 2 cups liquid yeast,
- 2 cups rolled oats,
- 2 teaspoons sugar,
- 1 teaspoon salt,
- 1 teaspoon butter.

Add white flour as long as you can stir in; beat well; let rise over night; stir up well in the morning; and add one cup of chopped or ground peanuts; pour into buttered baking-pan and set in a warm place to rise; when light bake in a moderate oven for one hour.

### NO. 13, PEANUT BREAD NUMBER THREE

A delicious loaf can be made by adding half pint of finely-ground nuts to every loaf of bread when baking. Add the nuts when the bread is worked down the last time.

### NO. 14, PEANUT ROLLS NUMBER ONE

- 2 cups of soft, white bread-crumbs,
- 4 tablespoons peanut butter,
- ½ cupful grated coconut, chopped fine,
- 1 salt spoon celery seed,
- 1 teaspoon salt,
- 1 well beaten egg,
- ½ pound blanched and ground peanuts.

Mix thoroughly; make into rolls, and fry in deep fat or bake in an over; serve with nut sauce.

### NO. 15, PEANUT ROLLS NUMBER TWO

Make the dough exactly the same as for Parker House rolls. At the last working add a heaping teaspoon of ground peanuts, and work into each roll.

### NO. 16, SWEDISH NUT ROLLS

- 1 pint milk, scalded,
- ½ cup butter,
- ¼ cup sugar,
- 1 scant teaspoon salt,
- 2 eggs (white),
- ½ cup yeast, 7 or 8 cups flour.

Mix early in the morning a sponge with the milk, sugar, salt, eggs, and yeast, using flour enough to make a drop batter. Place in a pan of warm water, and when light add the butter (softened) and enough more flour to thicken it. Knead well, and let it rise again. When light roll out into a large triangular piece of third of an inch thick. Spread all over with soft butter and a sprinkling of sugar, cinnamon, and a generous coating of finely-ground peanuts. Roll over and over; cut off slices an inch thick; lay them on a well-buttered pan with the cut-side down. Let it rise again, and bake in a moderate oven.

### NO. 17, PEANUT COOKIES NUMBER ONE

- 3 cups flour,
- 2 eggs,
- 1 cup sugar,
- 1½ cups ground peanuts,
- ½ cup butter,
- 1 cup sweet milk,
- 1 teaspoon baking powder.

Cream butter and sugar; add eggs well beaten; now add the milk and flour; flavor to taste with vanilla; and the peanuts last; drop one spoonful to the cooky in well-greased pans; bake quickly.

### NO. 18, PEANUT COOKIES NUMBER TWO

- 4 teaspoons butter,
- 1 cup sugar,
- 2 eggs, well beaten,
- 2 teaspoons baking powder,
- 2 cups flour,
- 1 cup ground peanuts,

Sweet milk sufficient to make a stiff batter. Drop on well-greased tins and bake quickly.

## NO. 19, PEANUT COOKIES NUMBER THREE

- 1/3 cup butter,
- ½ cup sugar,
- 2 eggs well beaten,
- ½ cup flour,
- 1 teaspoon baking powder,
- 1 cup blanched and finely-chopped peanuts,
- 1 teaspoon lemon juice.

Sweeten milk enough to make a stiff batter. Cream the butter and add the sugar and eggs well beaten. Sift the flour and baking powder together. Add the butter, sugar and flour; then add the milk, nuts and lemon juice. Drop from a spoon on an unbuttered baking sheet; sprinkle with chopped nuts, and bake in a very slow oven.

## NO. 20, PEANUT TEA ROLLS (DELICIOUS)

- 2 cups raised sponge,
- 1 cup sugar,
- ½ cup butter,
- 1 cup ground peanuts.

Take two cups of sponge, the sugar, melted butter, eggs, peanuts, and salt to taste. Mix thoroughly; knead in enough flour to make dough as for rolls. Set in a warm place to rise; when light shape into rolls; let rise until twice their size; rub melted butter over the top with a small paint brush; then sift sugar and ground peanuts over the top.

## NO. 21, PEANUT BARS

- 2 cups flour,
- 1 cup coarsely-chopped peanuts,
- ½ cup sugar,
- 2 tablespoons butter,
- 1 teaspoon baking powder,

- ½ cup milk,
- 1 egg, pinch of salt.

Sift flour, salt and baking powder into a bowl; rub in the butter, nuts and sugar; mix to a rather stiff dough with the egg and milk; turn on to a floured board, and roll out two-thirds of an inch thick, cut into bars of convenient size, and fry in the fat until golden brown.

### NO. 22, PEANUT WAFERS NUMBER ONE

- 2 cups flour,
- 1 cup water,
- 1 cup sugar, (powdered),
- ½ cup rolled peanuts,
- ½ cup butter.

Rub the butter and sugar together until light and craemy; add the flour and water alternately. Lastly add the peanuts; drop on buttered tins, and bake quickly. Cut in squares while hot, as it soon gets brittle after cooling.

### NO. 23, PEANUT WAFERS NUMBER TWO

- ¼ cup butter,
- 1 cup flour,
- 1 cup sugar,
- 1 cup blanched nuts,
- 1 egg.

Grind or roll the nuts; stir into butter; drop on buttered tins, and bake quickly.

### NO. 24, PEANUT WAFERS NUMBER THREE

- 3 tablespoons flour,
- ½ teaspoon baking powder,
- 2 well-beaten eggs,

- ½ brown sugar,
- 1 cupful ground peanuts.

Mix thoroughly; drop on buttered paper, and bake slowly to a light brown.

### NO. 25, PEANUT MUFFINS NUMBER ONE

- ½ cupful chopped peanuts,
- 2 eggs beaten very light,
- ½ teaspoon soda, dissolved in tablespoon of water,
- ½ pint thick sour buttermilk,
- ½ teaspoon salt,
- 1½ cupfulls flour, or enough to make a stiff batter.

Add soda to the sour milk; stir well; make the batter quickly; when ready to drop into the pans add peanuts; bake in a quick oven from 20 to 25 minutes.

### NO. 26, PEANUT MUFFINS NUMBER TWO

Use the above recipe, and in addition add ½ cupful of cold, cooked rice. Chopped figs, dates, etc., make very pleasing variations.

### NO. 27, PEANUT DOUGHNUTS NUMBER ONE

- 2 eggs, beaten light,
- 1 cup sugar,
- 3 tablespoons melted butter,
- 1 cup sour milk,
- 4 cups flour,
- ½ teaspoon soda,
- 1 saltspoon salt,
- 1 saltspoon cinnamon,
- 1 cup finely-ground or chopped peanuts.

Into the well-beaten eggs stir the sugar, butter, milk, and nuts; add flour to make a dough just stiff enough to roll out; roll, cut out, and fry in deep fat hot enough for the dough to rise at once.

## NO. 28, PEANUT DOUGHNUTS NUMBER TWO

- 1 pint sweet milk,
- 1 cup sugar,
- ½ cup butter (softened),
- 2/3 cut yeast,
- 1 egg, well beaten,
- 1 tablespoon lemon juice,
- 5½ to 6 cups flour,
- 1 pint chopped peanuts.

Mix in the order given; rise slowly till light; roll out and cut in shape; rise quickly until very light, then fry in hot fat.

## CAKES
## NO. 29, PEANUT CAKE NUMBER ONE

- ¼ lb. butter,
- 2 cups flour,
- 4 eggs (white only) well beaten,
- ¾ cup water,
- 1 cup finely-ground peanuts,
- 1 teaspoon baking powder.

Beat the sugar and butter to a cream; add the water and flour; stir until smooth; add half the well-beaten whites, then the nuts, then the remainder of the whites and the baking powder; pour into square, flat pans lined with greased paper to a depth of three inches, and bake in a moderate oven for 45 or 50 minutes.

## NO. 30, PEANUT CAKE NUMBER TWO

- 9 ounces flour,

- 4 ounces butter,
- 3 ounces chopped peanuts,
- 4 eggs,
- 1 teaspoon vanilla,
- ¼ teaspoon salt,
- 1 teaspoon baking powder.

Sift flour, salt and baking powder together; cream the butter and sugar; add the vanilla, chopped nuts, and yolks of the eggs well beaten; add flour, then whipped whites, and beat well; bake in shallow pan in medium oven; when cold, ice with boiled icing.

### NO. 31, PEANUT ROLL CAKE WITH JELLY

- 4 eggs,
- 2/3 cup powdered sugar,
- ¼ teaspoon salt,
- ½ teaspoon baking powder.

Beat egg yolks and sugar till light; add mixed dry ingredients, then stiffly beaten whites; mix lightly together. Bake in thin sheet in a quick oven. As soon as done turn quickly on a towel wrung out of water; spread with jelly; springle liberally with coarsely-chopped peanuts; roll up and dust with powdered sugar.

### NO. 32, PEANUT LAYER CAKE

Make cake exactly the same as for roll cake, except bake in jelly-cake tins. Make the pastry cream as follows:

- 2 cups sugar,
- 1½ pints milk,
- 3 tablespoons corn starch,
- 1 tablespoon butter,
- 2 teaspoons extract of lemon,
- 1 pint coarsely-ground peanuts."

Add peanuts to the milk, let simmer 5 minutes; with sugar add the starch dissolved in a little cold water; as soon as it reboils take from the fire; beat in the yolks; return to the fire two or three minutes to set the eggs; when cold spread between the layers of cake, and finish with clear icing garnished with blanched peanuts.

### NO. 33, METROPOLITAN CAKE WITH PEANUTS

- 1 cup granulated sugar,
- 1½ cups butter,
- ½ cup milk,
- 2½ cups well-sifted flour,
- 2 teaspoons baking powder, sifted with the flour,
- 2 cupfuls chopped peanuts and citron mixed,
- 4 eggs (white).

Cream the butter and sugar; flour nuts and citron before adding; bake 45 minutes in a moderate oven; flavor icing with lemon extract, and garnish top with split peanuts and pecan meats.

### NO. 34, PEANUT CAKE WITH MOLASSES

- 2 cups molasses,
- 1 cup brown sugar,
- 1 cup lard,
- 2 cups hot water,
- 4 cups flour,
- 1 pint ground peanuts,
- 2 teaspoons cinnamon,
- ½ teaspoon cloves,
- ¼ nutmeg, grated,
- 1 heaping teaspoon soda,
- 1 egg.

Mix the peanuts, spices, and soda with the flour; heap the measure of flour slightly; mix the molasses, sugar, lard, and water; stir in the flour; add the beaten egg last. Bake in shallow dripping-pan, and sprinkle with powdered sugar just before putting in the oven.

### NO. 35, PEANUT PUDDING

- 1 cup molasses,
- ½ cup butter,
- 1 cup hot water,
- 3 cups flour,
- 1 teaspoon soda,
- ½ teaspoon coarsely-ground peanuts,
- ½ teaspoon ground cloves, mix and steam two hours.
- Sauce for same:
- 1 tablespoon butter,
- ½ cup sugar,
- 1 teaspoon flour.

"Mix all to a cream; pour over this enough boiling water to make it like cream; flavor to suit taste.

### NO. 36, PEANUT STRIPS WITH BANANAS

- 2 cups mashed banana pulp,
- 1 cup oat flakes,
- 1 cup flour,
- 1 cup peanut meal,
- 1 cup sugar,
- ½ cup (softened) butter
- 1 saltspoon (or more) of salt.

Blend all together; roll out ¼ of an inch thick; cut in stripes and bake in a quick oven.

### MISCELLANEOUS DISHES FROM PEANUTS

### NO. 38, MOCK CHICKEN

Blanch and grind a sufficient number of peanuts until they are quite oily; stir in one well-beaten egg, if too thin, thicken with rolled bread crumbs or cracker dust; stir in little salt. Boil some sweet potatoes until done; peel and cut in thin slices; spread generously with peanut mixture; dip in white of egg; fry to a chicken brown; serve hot.

## NO. 39, MOCK VEAL CUTLETS

Wash one cup of lentils, and soak over night; in the morning strain and parboil in fresh boiling water for 30 minutes; drain again, and cook until soft in sufficient boiling water to cover them; rub through a sieve, and to the puree add ¼ cup of melted butter, 1 cup of fine Graham bread crumbs, 1 cup of blanched and chopped peanuts, 1 tablespoon each of grated celery and minced onion; season with ¼ teaspoon of mixed herbs, salt, and pepper; blend all thoroughly together, and for minto cutlets; dip these in egg and then in fine bread-crumbs; place in a well-greased baking pan, and brown in quick oven; arrange around a mound of well seasoned mashed potatoes, and serve with brown sauce.

## NO. 40, PEANUT PATTIES

- 1 pint toasted bread crumbs rolled fine,
- 1 pint mashed potatoes (white or sweet),
- 2 teaspoons baking powder dissolved in the yolks of two eggs.

Season with salt, pepper, sage and mace; heat all together; form into cakes; dip each cake into the whites of the eggs, then into peanut meal, and brown lightly in a frying-pan containing a little pork fat, not deep fat; turn and brown on both sides.

## NO. 41, BROWN SAUCE

Mix thoroughly 1 teaspoon of peanut butter and 2 tablespoons browned flour with 1 tablespoon cream; add gradually 2 cups hot milk, and stir and cook until the mixture thickens; just before serving add 4 tablespoons strained tomatoes, and a little salt and pepper.

### NO. 42, PEANUT SAUSAGES

Grind ½ pound of roasted peanuts, ½ pound pecans, 1 ounce hickory nuts, and ½ pound walnut meats. Mix with six very ripe bananas; pack in a mould, and steam continuously for two hours; when done remove lid of kettle or mould, and when mixture is cold turn out and serve the same as roast meat sliced thin for sandwiches, or with cold tomato sauce or other sauce.

### NO. 43, PEANUT AND CHEESE ROAST

- 1 cup grated cheese,
- 1 cup finely-ground peanuts,
- 1 cup bread crumbs, juice of ½ lemon,
- 1 teaspoon chopped onion,
- 1 tablespoon butter, salt and pepper to taste.

Cook the onion in the butter and a little water until it is tender. Mix the other ingredients, and moisten with water, using the water in which the onion has been cooked. Pour into a shallow baking dish and brown in the oven.

### NO. 44, PEANUT OMELET

Cream a slice of bread in half a cup of rich malk; beat the whites and yolks of two eggs separately; add the yolks to the bread-crumbs and milk; to half a cup of finely-ground peanuts add a dash of pepper and salt; mix thoroughly; fold in the whites, and cook as usual in a buttered pan.

### NO. 45, BAKED PEANUTS WITH RICE

- 4 cups milk,

- ½ cup rice,
- 1 cup coarsely-ground peanuts,
- 1/3 cup sugar,
- 1 tablespoon lemon juice,
- ½ teaspoon salt.

Wash rice, putting a layer of rice and a layer of peanuts into a well-buttered pudding-dish until all is used; mix the salt and sugar, sprinkling each layer with it; finish with a layer of peanuts on top, pour on the milk, if it does not cover the rice put in sufficient water; bake three hours in a very slow oven; add hot water if it cooks too dry.

## NO. 46, PEANUT MACARONI

- 1 cup broken macaroni,
- 2 quarts boiling salted water,
- 1 cup rich milk,
- 2 tablespoons flour,
- ¼ to ½ lb. cheese,
- ½ teaspoon salt,
- 1 cup coarsely ground peanuts.

Cook macaroni in the boiling salted water; a dash of cayenne pepper; drain in a strainer, and pour cold water over it to keep the pieces from sticking together; mince cheese, and mix with all other ingredients except the macaroni; put sauce and macaroni in alternate layers in a well-buttered baking dish; cover with buttered crumbs, and bake slowly until crumbs are brown.

## NO. 47, PEANUT PIE CRUST

Add at the rate of 1 tablespoon of finely-ground peanuts to one pie-crust. You will be pleased with the agreeable change in pie-crusts or any other pastry.

## NO. 48, PEANUT BREAKFAST CAKES

Mash 2 cups of well-cooked, split peas or beans; press through a sieve; add 1 teaspoon grated celery, 1 teaspoon minced onion, 1 cup of milk, 1 cup soft bread crumbs, 1 tablespoon butter, 1 cup crushed peanuts, 1 well-beaten egg, season with salt and pepper; form into small flat cakes, and brown in hot fat; place a nicely-poached egg on each cake; garnish with parsley, and serve with hot cream or brown sauce.

## NO. 49, PEANUTS AND MUSHROOMS

Cook 2 tablespoons of chopped onion and ½ cup chopped fresh mushrooms in 4 tablespoons of butter for five or six minutes; stir in 2 tablespoons flour, a little salt and pepper, and 1 ½ cups milk; cook and stir the while for five minutes longer; then add 1 cup finely-chopped peanuts, re-heat, and boil slowly for 10 minutes; serve on squares of buttered toast.

## NO. 50, PEANUT TIMBALES

- ½ pint of peanuts cooked until soft in salted water; drain and mash,
- 2 well-beaten eggs and two cups thin cream, added to the nuts,
- ½ teaspoon salt, and a dash of pepper.

Turn into custard cups; put the cups in a basin; surround them with boiling water; cover the tops with buttered paper, and bake in a moderate oven for 20 or 25 minutes; then unmould and serve with a little cream sauce poured around them.

## NO. 51, PEANUT BUTTER

Shell the peanuts; roast just enough so that the hulls will slip off easily; remove all the hulls gently rolling, fanning, and screening; grind very fine in any sort of mill, passing through several times if necessary; pack in cans, bottles or jars, and seal if not for immediate use. Some manufacturers add a little salt and a small amount of olive oil; others do not, according to taste. For small quantities of butter a good meat-grinder will answer the purpose. If the nuts are ground fine enough no additional oil will be necessary.

### NO. 52, PEANUT STUFFING NUMBER ONE

Crumble pint of corn bread, adding to it a grated rind of one lemon, a cup of finely-chopped peanuts, two tablespoons of mixed, dried herbs, salt and pepper to taste, and one-half cup of melted butter. Bacon drippings may be used instead of butter.

### NO. 53, PEANUT STUFFING NUMBER TWO

- ½ pint shelled and roasted peanuts (peanut meal can be used).
- 4 drops onion juice,
- 1 teaspoon chopped parsley, slightly moistened with cream,
- ½ teaspoon powdered herbs, Season highly with salt and pepper.

### NO. 54, PEANUT STUFFING NUMBER THREE

- 2 cups hot mashed potatoes,
- 1 teaspoon onion juice or grated onion,
- ½ cup ground peanuts (peanut meal is excellent).
- ¼ teaspoon paprika,
- 1 teaspoon salt,
- 4 tablespoons thick cream,
- 1 tablespoon butter,
- 2 eggs (yolks)

One teaspoon of sweet herbs if desired. Blend all together, and stuff in the usual way.

### NO. 55, PEANUT MEAL NUMBER ONE

Blanch the peanuts and grind very fine but not sufficient to become too oily. This meal is especially fine as a substitute in making almond macaroons and small cakes, to which it imparts the desired almond flavor, and is much cheaper than the almond meal.

### NO. 56, BROWN PEANUT MEAL

Roast the peanuts carefully without scorching; when a rich light-brown rub off the hulls and grind the same as for No. 49. This meal has many uses, such as soups, gravies, cakes, candies, etc.

### NO. 57, CREAM PEANUTS

- 1 pint white crowder peas,
- 1 cup cream,
- 1 pint peanuts,
- 1 teaspoon sugar,
- ½ teaspoon pepper,
- 1 saltspoon salt.

Boil the peas until thoroughly done; pass through a colander; grind or crush the blanched peanuts; add all the ingredients except the cream and nuts; boil thirty minutes; mix cream and nuts together with a tablespoon of flour; mix thoroughly; stir into the boiling peas; boil five minutes; whip vigorously until light, and serve. If one spoonful of flour is not sufficient add more.

### NO. 58, SALTED PEANUTS

Roast the peanuts; shell, and remove the thin hulls; put in a pan, butter slightly; put in over and heat through; spread on piece of white paper; sprinkle with fine salt, and serve.

Note.--If the nuts are very greasy allow them to drain before applying the salt.

## NO. 59, PEANUT BUTTER SANDWICHES

Roast the desired number of peanuts; rub the thin hull off the nuts; grind or rub in a mortar until quite smooth and oily; salt to taste, and spread a thin layer between crackers, lunch biscuits, rolls, or bread of that character. If the butter is not as thin as you wish add a little fresh cow's butter, a little milk or water, and rub well. This will not keep as well as when the milk or butter is left out.

## SALADS

## NO. 60, PEANUT SALAD NUMBER ONE

- 1 small cabbage,
- 1 teaspoon flour,
- 2 teaspoon salt,
- 1 teaspoon mustard,
- 1 teaspoon sugar,
- 1 cup vinegar,
- ½ teaspoon pepper,
- 2 eggs,
- 1 pint peanuts.

Chop cabbage and peanuts up fine; add the salt and pepper; cream the butter, mustard, sugar, and flour together; stir in the vinegar; cook in double boiler until stiff; add yolks of the eggs; pour over nuts and cabbage, and serve.

## NO. 61, PEANUT SALAD NUMBER TWO

- 1 cup roasted peanuts,
- 1 cup sour apples,
- Chop the nuts and apples together,
- Make a dressing of--
- ½ cup water,
- ½ cup sugar,
- 2 tablespoons butter,

- ½ cup vinegar,
- 1 tablespoon flour,
- 1 egg.

Whip all together, and let boil long enough to thicken; then pour over salad; serve on crisp lettuce leaves.

### NO. 62, PEANUT SALAD NUMBER THREE

Blanch peanuts; put in the oven and brown with a bit of butter and a sprinkle of salt; when cold chop coarsely. To each cupful of nuts add two cups of finely-shredded celery and an equal amount of sour apples; mix thoroughly, serve on lettuce leaves with mayonnaise dressing.

### NO. 63, PEANUT AND DATE SALAD

- 2 cup dates, stoned and cut into small pieces,
- ½ cup coarsely-ground peanuts,
- 2 cups celery, finely cut.

Stir well, then mix with cream salad dressing.

### NO. 64, PEANUT SALAD WITH BANANAS

Slice balanas through center; spread out on lettuce leaves, and sprinkle liberally with chopped peanuts; serve with mayonnaise or plain salad dressing.

### ICE CREAM

### NO. 65, PEANUT ICE CREAM NUMBER ONE

- 1 pint peanuts,
- 2 quarts milk,
- 2 cups sugar,

- 1 pint cream,
- 3 eggs,
- 2 teaspoons vanilla.

Roast, shell, and roll the peanuts until they are quite fine; brown one cup of sugar and add to the milk; next add the remainder of sugar. The cream, vanilla, and lastly the peanuts; freeze.

### NO. 66, PEANUT CREAM NUMBER TWO

Make a quart of lemon or vanilla cream by the usual rule; when this half frozen take out the dasher and add ½ pound of peanut brittle, or two or three bars of peanut candy previously put through the meat chopper. The result is a light-brown cream tasting like caramel, with the nuts all through it. It may be served in glasses or put in a brick.

### NO. 67, PEANUT CREAM (PROFESSIONAL WAY)

Take 21 pounds of 18 per cent cream, 4 pounds granulated sugar, 1 teaspoon peanut butter dissolved in ½ cup boiling water; add caramel to give the light-brown hue desired; freeze in the ordinary way. This gives only a pleasing suggestion of peanut flavor. If more is desired increase the quantity of butter or add peanut meal.

### NO. 68, PEANUT FRAPPE

Make 1 pint of good gelatine; set aside to harden. Stir 1 cup granulated sugar into 1 pint of whipped cream; when the gelatine is just on the point of setting stir into it the whipped cream by beating with a fork; add 3/4 cup of peanut meal; serve in sherbet glasses with fresh or preserved fruit.

### NO. 69, PEANUT AND PRUNE ICE CREAM

- 2 cups milk,

- 3 eggs (yolks),
- ½ pound pulp from well-cooked and sweetened prunes,
- 1 quart cream,
- ½ cup blanched and ground peanuts. (Peanut meal can be used),
- 1 teaspoon vanilla extract and a pinch of salt.

Heat the milk; pour it into the well-beaten egg yolks; blend all the other ingredients thoroughly; freeze and serve in dainty glasses.

## CANDIES AND CONFECTIONS

### NO. 70, PEANUT-BUTTER CANDY

- 2 cups sugar,
- ½ cup milk,
- 2 tablespoons peanut butter.

Blend together; boil for five minutes; remove from the fire and heat steadily until cool.

### NO. 71, PEANUT CANDY

- 2 cups sugar,
- 1 cup peanuts.

Melt the sugar in a frying pan, melt slowly, stirring constantly until melted; butter a shallow dish, and cover bottom with the roasted and cleaned nuts; pour the candy over them; set aside; when cool break in pieces, and serve.

### NO. 72, PEANUT CARAMELS

- 1 cup sugar,
- 1 cup molasses,
- 1 cup butter,

- 1 cup milk or cream,
- 1 cup ground peanuts.

Cream sugar and butter; add molasses, cream or milk, stirring constantly; put mixture into a boiler and let boil, gently scraping the bottom to prevent burning (do not stir); let cook until it forms a soft mass when dropped into cool water; add peanuts and pour into buttered tins. The layer should not be more than ½ an inch thick. When cool enough cut into small squares, and wrap in thin glazed paper.

## NO. 73, PEANUT KISSES

- 1 egg (white)
- 1 cupful sifted brown sugar,
- 1 cupful chopped peanuts,
- ¼ teaspoon vanilla.

Beat the egg-white very stiff; stir in the sugar, nuts, and vanilla, and drop on a buttered pan; make the kisses two inches apart; bake in a moderate oven.

## NO. 74, PEANUT CHOCOLATE TAFFY

- ½ pound of sweet chocolate,
- 2 cups granulated sugar,
- ¼ teaspoon cream of tartar.
- ½ cup boiling water,
- ½ cup of peanut meal or coarsely ground meats, as desired.

Grate the chocolate; add the boiling water; stir until dissolved. Place the kettle over the fire, and cook for several minutes; add the peanuts, and boil until the candy will snap when pulled apart, remove from the fire, and pour out to cool; pull and cut as desired.

## NO. 75, PEANUT BALLS

- 2 cups brown sugar,
- 1 cup New Orleans molasses,
- ½ cup water,
- ¼ (scant) teaspoon cream of tartar.

Boil all together until the candy will snap when tested in cold water; remove from the fire; add two cups blanched peanuts (coarsely broken; stir until nearly cold; form into balls by rolling between palms of the hands; wrap in paraffin paper to prevent sticking together.

### NO. 76, PEANUT CANDY NUMBER TWO

- 2 cups brown sugar,
- 1 cup rich milk,
- ¼ cup syrup,
- 1 tablespoon butter,
- 1 cup shelled peanuts.

Mix sugar, milk, and butter; boil until a soft ball can be formed by dropping in cold water; when nearly cold beat, and add nuts.

### NO. 77, PEANUT FILLING FOR CAKES, COOKIES, ETC.

- 3 teaspoons corn starch,
- 2 eggs (yolks),
- ½ cup rich milk,
- ½ cup sugar,
- 1 cup chopped peanut meats,
- ½ cup water.

Use double boiler; put in the water and milk; when hot stir in 3 teaspoons corn starch previously dissolved in a little cold water; cook for 10 minutes; add the beaten yolks of 2 eggs that have been creamed with ½ cup sugar; cook for 3 minutes; when cold add the chopped nuts; flavor with lemon or vanilla.

## NO. 78, CANDIED PEANUTS

- 3 cups sugar,
- 1 cup water.

Boil until it hardens when dropped in water; then flavor with lemon. It must not boil after the lemon is put in. Put a nut on end of a fine knitting needle; dip; take out and turn until cold. If the candy gets cold set on a warm stove for a few minutes.

## NO. 79, PEANUT NOUGAT WITH HONEY

- 3/8 cup honey,
- ½ cup brown sugar,
- 1 pound blanched peanuts,
- 2 eggs (white).

Boil the honey and sugar together until drops of the mixture hold their shape when poured into cold water; add whites of the two eggs, well beaten, and cook very slowly, stirring constantly until the mixture becomes brittle when dropped in cold water; add the peanuts and cool under a weight, break in pieces or cut and wrap in waxed paper.

## NO. 80, PEANUT BUTTER FUDGE

- 2 cups powdered sugar,
- 1 cup milk,
- 2 heaping teaspoons peanut butter.

Mix ingredients; boil vigorously five minutes; beat; pour in a buttered pan, and cut in squares.

## NO. 81, PEANUT DIVINITY FUDGE

- 2½ cups sugar,

- ½ cup syrup,
- ½ cup water,
- 2 eggs,
- 1 cup coarsely-broken peanuts.

Boil the sugar, syrup and water together until, when dropped on cold water, the mixture will form a hard ball between the fingers; beat the eggs stiff; pour half of the boiling mixture over eggs, beating constantly; return remaining half of the mixture to the stove, and boil until it forms a hard ball when dropped into cold water; remove from the stove, and pour slowly into first half, beating constantly; add peanuts, and flavor with vanilla; pour into a buttered pan, and cut into squares.

## NO. 82, PEANUT CHOCOLATE FUDGE

- 2 cups white granulated sugar,
- 1 tablespoon butter,
- 1 cup cream,
- ¼ cake unsweetened chocolate,
- 1 cup chopped peanuts.

Put in the sugar and cream, and when this becomes hot put in the chocolate, broken up into fine pieces; stir vigorously and constantly, put in the butter when it begins to boil; stir until it creams when beaten on a saucer; remove and beat until quite cool, and pour into buttered tins; add the nuts before stirring.

## NO. 83, PEANUT BRITTLE NUMBER ONE

- 3 cups granulated sugar,
- 1 scant cup boiling water,
- 1 cup roasted peanuts,
- ¼ teaspoon soda.

Melt all together over a slow fire; cook gently without stirring until a little hardens when dropped in cold water; add the nuts; turn the mixture into well buttered pans and cut while hot. Stirring will cause the syrup to sugar.

## NO. 84, PEANUT BRITTLE NUMBER TWO

- 2 cups granulated sugar,
- 1 cup freshly roasted peanuts.

Shell and clean the peanuts; put in the stove to heat, put sugar in frying pan, and heat over a hot fire until it is changed to caramel; put the peanuts in a well-buttered tin; pour the sugar over them at once; when cold turn the pan up-side down, and tap bottom until the candy falls out; break into small pieces.

## NO. 85, PEANUT AND POPCORN BALLS

- ½ teaspoon soda,
- 1 pint syrup,
- 2 tablespoons butter,
- 1 teaspoon vinegar,
- 3 quarts fresh popcorn,
- 1 quart freshly-roasted peanuts.

Cook until the syrup hardens when a little is dropped in cold water; remove to back of stove; add the soda dissolved in a teaspoon of hot water; pour syrup over the corn and nuts, stirring until each kernel is well coated; mould into balls.

## NO. 86, FROSTED PEANUT FUDGE

Make a good chocolate fudge; beat until creamy; pour into a well-buttered pan of about one inch depth; when nearly hard, cover with finely-chopped fig preserves; then place in a kettle 1 cup of granulated sugar, ¼ cup water, and a pinch of cream of tartar, boil until it forms a hard ball when dropped into water, pour the stiffly beaten white of one egg, add one teaspoon lemon juice or extract;

cover fruit with a generous layer of crushed peanuts; whip syrup until creamy; pour over the fruit; when cold cut into squares.

### NO. 87, PEANUT PANOCHA

- 2 cups brown sugar,
- 3/4 cup cream,
- 1 teaspoon vanilla,
- 2 tablespoons butter,
- 1 cup chopped peanuts.

Boil all the ingredients together except the vanilla and nuts until the soft-ball stage is reached; remove from the fire and let cool; add the vanilla and nuts; beat until creamy; turn into a buttered pan; when cool cut into squares.

### NO. 88, PEANUT FRUIT ROLL

- 3¼ cups sugar,
- 1 cup cream,
- 1/3 cup coarsely-chopped peanuts,
- ½ cup each of figs, dates and candied pineapple.

Boil sugar and cream until it reaches the soft-ball stage; pour out on a large platter, and cool, work with a wooden spoon until creamy; add the nuts and fruit; work until mass begins to stiffen; then make into a long roll, and wrap in moist towel. In an hour or more it can be sliced, and the slices wrapped in oiled paper.

### NO. 89, SULTANA PEANUT CARAMELS

- 1 cup light brown sugar,
- ½ cup golden corn syrup,
- 1 tablespoon butter,
- 1 teaspoon vanilla extract,
- 1 cup granulated sugar,
- ½ cup milk,

- ½ cup coarsely-chopped peanuts,
- 1 cup sultana raisins.

Place the ingredients in a sauce-pan, and boil to the firm ball stage; remove from the fire, and flavor with the vanilla. These are especially nice when dipped in chocolate.

### NO. 90, NUT HONEY

- 1 pound honey,
- 1 pound sugar,
- 1 tablespoon water.

Mix and set in a vessel of hot water until melted; cook over a moderate fire until it forms a ball when a little is dropped in cold water; add one pint of crushed peanuts; flavor with lemon, cut into squares.

### NO. 91, PEANUT ALMOND FUDGE (VERY FINE)

- 1 cup peanuts deeply browned but not scorched.
- crush or grind,
- 1½ cups sugar,
- 1 cup milk,
- 1 tablespoon butter,
- 1 teaspoon almond extract.

Brown ½ cup of sugar in a granite pan, add the milk, when the brown sugar is thoroughly dissolved add one cup of granulated sugar and the butter; boil to the soft-ball stage, flavor with the extract; add the peanuts; beat until creamy; pour into buttered tins, make off into squares.

### NO. 92, PEANUT TUTTI-FRUITTI CARAMELS

- ½ cup raisins, seeded and chopped,
- ½ cup preserved watermelon rind, chopped very fine,

- ¼ cup chopped figs,
- 2 cups light brown sugar,
- ½ cup milk,
- ¼ cup candied pineapple,
- 1 cup peanuts, blanched and ground,
- 1 cup corn syrup,
- 1 tablespoon butter,
- 1 teaspoon lemon extract.
- ¼ teaspoon soda.

Place all the ingredients in a sauce-pan together, and boil to the hard stage: stir only enough to keep the mixture from sticking. If the double boiler is used the candy will not stick much. Remove from the fire; add the extract; pour into buttered pans, and mark off into squares.

### NO. 93, PEANUT HONEY PUFFS

- 1 cup cream,
- 3 cups sugar,
- ¼ cup honey,
- 1 egg (white),
- 1 cup ground peanuts.

Boil the cream and sugar (without stirring) until the threading stage is reached; add the honey; when syrup will make a soft-ball when dropped into cold water, remove from the fire and beat into it the well-whipped white of an egg; add the nut-meats; when firm and creamy whip into balls.

### NO. 94, PEANUT MAPLE-SUGAR FUDGE

- 2 cups maple sugar, in cold water; add the nut-meats; remove from the fire, and stir
- 1 cup milk,
- 1 cup chopped peanuts,
- 1 tablespoon butter.

Boil the sugar, milk, and butter to a soft-ball when tested until creamy; pour into buttered pans; when cool cut into squares.

## NO. 95, PEANUT CARROT FUDGE

- 1 cup carrot pulp,
- 1 cup corn syrup,
- ½ cup peanut meal,
- 1 teaspoon vanilla or almond extract,
- 2 cups sugar,
- 1 tablespoon butter,
- 1 lemon,
- 1 orange.

Bake some nice, yellow carrots until tender; pass through a sieve; to a cupful of this pulp add all the ingredients except the extract; pour into buttered pans, and when cool cut into cubes; use both the juice and half the grated peel of the lemon and orange.

## NO. 96, PEANUT AND FIG CANDY

- 1 pound sugar,
- ½ teaspoon vinegar,
- ½ pint water,
- ½ pint chopped peanut meats.

Boil over a slow fire the sugar, water, and vinegar until it forms a hard ball when tasted; stir a few times; shred the same quantity of dried figs as peanuts; mix with the peanuts; spread out in a well-buttered dish; pour the hot syrup over them; cool, and cut or break into small pieces.

## NO. 97, PEANUT NOUGAT

- 1 cup peanut meal,
- 1/8 teaspoon salt,
- 1 cup granulated sugar.

Put sugar in frying pan; stir over slow fire; when melted add the peanut meal; mix thoroughly; butter knives and the under-side of a pan; sprinkle generously with whole or half nuts roasted to a delicate brown; shape into squares ½ inch thick. Arrange it so that each square contains one or two whole or half nuts.

### NO. 98, PEANUT MARSHMALLOWS

- ½ pound gum Arabic dissolved in 1 pint of water,
- ½ pound granulated sugar,
- 4 eggs, whites, well beaten,
- Lemon flavoring to taste,
- ½ cup peanut meal.

Strain the gum Arabic; add the sugar; stir over a slow fire until dissolved; cook to the consistency of thick honey; remove from the fire, and stir in the egg whites; stir until it is somewhat thin and does not adhere to the fingers; add the lemon; pour in tins dusted with corn starch; put in cool place; when firm cut into small squares.

### NO. 99, PEANUT TAFFY CANDY

- 1 cup sugar,
- ½ cup molasses,
- ¼ cup butter,
- 1 cup peanuts (freshly-roasted peanuts-rolled).

Boil the sugar, molasses and butter together until it snaps when dropped in cold water; remove from fire; stir in the mashed peanuts; pour in buttered dish; pull when cold enough.

### NO. 100, PEANUT BROWNIES

- 1 cup sugar,
- ½ cup flour,
- ½ cup melted butter,
- ½ cup coarsely-ground peanuts,

- 2 eggs,
- 1 square of chocolate.

Mix and bake in shallow pan in a quick oven; garnish the top with nuts; cut in squares.

## FANCY CHEESE FOR THE HOME

## CREAM CHEESE (After M. R. Tolstrup).

Into a gallon of 10% to 15% sweet cream put one or two tablespoons starter, fresh buttermilk, or clean clabbered milk; stir gently, and heat to about 85 degrees Fahrenheit. Then add about 20 drops of rennet extract or its equivalent in rennet tablets. Dilute the rennet with cold water at least 10 times its own volume before it is added to the cream. Mix well in cream: cover up carefully so as to retain the heat; set aside for about three hours, when a soft curd will be formed. Spread a piece of cheese-cloth over the bowl and carefully dip the curd into it; let drain for a few minutes; tie ends of the cloth together, and hang up to drain, which will require from 12 to 24 hours. Do not shake or break curd any more than is necessary, or much fat will be lost.

"When sufficiently drained salt to taste. Mix well; wrap cloth around the cheese, put between two boards, and press lightly for a few hours. When it assumes a light mealy consistency it is ready to eat.

"If this cheese is to be marketed it must be put in glasses or 4-ounce packages, and wrapped in wax paper and tin foil, or it may be put in small 4 or 8-ounce paraffin paper boxes.

## NO. 101, PEANUT CREAM CHEESE WITH OLIVES

Remove the seed and mince one ounce of olives very fine; run through a meat mincer, and one ounce of peanuts freshly roasted and treated in the same way. To every pound of cheese add this olive and nut mixture. This is very dainty and appetizing.

## NO. 102, PEANUT CREAM CHEESE WITH PIMENTO

To every pound of cream cheese grind ½ ounce of pimento pepper and one ounce of peanuts in the same way as recommended for the above.

## NO. 103, PEANUT SANDWICH CHEESE

To each pound of cream cheese add two ounces of peanut meal; blend thoroughly.

## NO. 104, PEANUT COFFEE

- ½ cup peanuts,
- ½ cup wheat or rye,
- ½ cup cow peas,

Roast all to a rich coffee brown; grind and make as for postum. To those who like a cereal coffee, this will be quite acceptable, even delicious. To more or less habitual coffee-drinkers, one-third or one-half real coffee will make the above recipe more acceptable.

## NO. 105, SALTED PEANUTS

Parch, rub, and winnow out the bran hulls; put in pan with just a speck of butter; heat gently, shaking all the time; when buttered sprinkle over with fine salt.

The above recipes are only a few of the many ways in which this wholesome pea can be prepared for human consumption.

# CHAPTER XII.

# THE SWEET POTATO AND WAYS OF PREPARING IT

There are but few, if any of our staple crops receiving more attention than the sweet potato, and indeed rightfully so. The splendid service it rendered during the great World War in the saving of wheat flour, will not soon be forgotten. The 178 different and attractive products (to date, December 1928) made from it, are sufficient to convince the most skeptical that we are just beginning to discover the real value and marvelous possibilities of this splendid vegetable.

## HISTORY

It is said that early navigators of the sixteenth century recognized such a strong resemblance between the Irish potato and the sweet potato that they called them both by the same name.

They are not only botanically unlike, but the edible parts of each are in character and taste quite unlike. Botanically, the sweet potato belongs to the morning glory family (Convolvulacea), and has been given the technical name of Impomeabatatas.

## ORIGIN

The origin of the sweet potato is doubtful, although there is very strong evidence that it is distinctly American, as fifteen or sixteen known species of the genus Batatas are found in this country. The "Indian Potato," "Tuckakoc" and "Hog Potato" which grow abundantly in this county and throughout the South, are all species of this genus.

## VARIETIES

More than 11 so-called varieties make up the present list, in many of which there is a distinction without a well-defined difference. Since some varieties do well in one section and practically fail in others, I have thought wise to list none except those that have proved the most prolific and best with us. Table Varieties--Dooley Yam, Improved Dooley Yam, Triumph, Pumpkin Yam, Porto Rico, and Nancy Hall.

Varieties for Feeding Stock--These grow to a very large size and make a fine yield, but are not very sweet and rather inferior for table use, but for making flour, starch, tapioca, and many other of the sweet potato products, they are excellent and in some instances, preferable--White Bermuda, Red Nansemond, and Haiti Spanish.

## AS FOOD FOR MAN

As food for human consumption the sweet potato has been, and always will be, held in very high esteem, and its popularity will increase as we learn more about its many possibilities.

There is an idea prevalent that anybody can cook sweet potatoes. This is a very great mistake, and the many, many dishes of illy cooked potatoes that are placed before me as I travel over the South, prompt me to believe that these recipes will be of value. The above bulletin so aptly adds the following:

The delicate flavor of a sweet potato is lost if it is not cooked properly. Steaming develops and preserves the flavor better than boiling, and baking better than steaming. A sweet potato cooked quickly is not cooked. Time is an essential element. Twenty minutes may serve to bake a sweet potato so that a hungry man can eat it, but if the flavor is an object, it should be kept in the oven for an hour.

## NO. 1, BOILED OR STEAMED

Boil or steam like white potatoes and without breaking the skin. If boiled, pour off the water as soon as done, cover the pot with a cloth and let stand in the back part of the range a few minutes before serving.

## NO. 2, BAKED

Scrub with a brush and rinse with water until thoroughly clean. Bake like white potatoes, without breaking the skin. When done break the skin in one place in the form of a cross, forcing the meat partly out, cap with butter and serve."

"Potatoes from 1 to ½ inches in diameter, and from 5 to 6 inches long, are the most desirable for baking--the flavor seems to be far superior to the larger kinds, to the round or irregular sort.

## NO. 3, BAKED IN ASHES

In this method the sweetness and piquancy of the potato is brought out in a manner hardly obtainable in any other way. Select the same kind of potatoes as described above for baking; cover them with warm ashes to a depth of 4 inches, upon this place live coals and hot cinders; let bake slowly for at least two hours. Remove the ashes with a soft brush, and serve while hot with butter.

## NO. 4, FRIEND

Cut in slices lengthwise and fry in deep grease, same as white potatoes. Care must be taken not to allow to become hard and dry.

## NO. 5, CHIPS

Cut in thin, steam until nearly done, allow the surplus water to drain off or dry between napkins, fry in deep fat to a light brown. This makes a fine breakfast dish. A little salt adds to its flavor.

## NO. 6, PIE (EXTRA FINE)

Boil in skins. When tender, remove skins; mash and beat until light. To each pint of potatoes, add ½ pint of milk, ½ pint of cream and four well beaten eggs; add 1½ teacups of sugar (less if the potatoes are very sweet). Add spice, cinnamon and ginger taste; one ground clove will improve it. Bake with bottom crust only. The above is enough for five or six pies.

## NO. 7, SLICED POTATO PIE

Line a deep baking dish with a rich sheet of pastry. Parboil the number of potatoes desired. When two-thirds done remove the skins, slice lengthwise, very thin, cover the dish to a depth of 2 inches, sprinkle with ground all-spice and a dash of ginger, cloves and nutmeg. To a pie sufficient for six people, scatter around the top in small pieces a lump of butter the size of a hen's egg; add one teacupful of sugar and ½ teacupful of molasses. Add ½ pint of cream, dust a little flour over the top sparingly; cover with hot water, put on upper crust, crimp edges, and bake in a moderate oven until done. Serve hot, with or without sauce.

## NO. 8, GLACE NO. 1

'Boil and cut in halves, medium-sized sweet potatoes, lay evenly in braising pan, baste with syrup and butter warmed together, sprinkle lightly with brown sugar, put in hot oven till brown, and serve in the syrup.

## NO. 9, GLACE NO. 2

Cut in slices ½ inch thick, wash and place in deep sauce pan; spread with butter; season with a little grated nutmeg and salt; moisten with broth or water, cover and let simmer over a slow fire for three-fourths of an hour, turning the slices so that they will glace on both sides. Serve with drawn butter or other sauce.

## NO. 10, SWEET POTATO COBBLER

Prepare the potatoes the same as for No. 6. Proceed to fill the dish the same as for layer cake, rolling out the layer of dough quite thin and spreading the mixture on in layers about ¼ of an inch thick. Proceed until the dish is full; add to each layer just enough water to cook the layer of crust. Bake until thoroughly done, and serve hot with drawn butter or hard sauce.

## NO. 11, WITH ROAST BEEF NO. 1

Roast the beef and make a brown gravy. Take sweet potatoes of medium size, previously baked; remove the skin, and garnish the dish with the potatoes. Serve the potatoes with the beef.

## NO. 12, WITH ROAST PORK

Parboil the desired number of potatoes with the peelings on until nearly done; remove the peel; lay in the baking dish with the nearly done roast; cook until done, and serve with the pork.

## NO. 13, WITH ROAST PORK

Select a desirable piece of fresh pork; bake until nearly done; dip or pour off as much as the grease as possible; prepare the potatoes the same as for No. 12. Lay them in the gravy; and slightly brown, with the meat, until done.

## No. 14, BROILED

Steam, pare and cut in slices 3/8 of an inch thick; lay the slices in a double boiler; salt; cover with melted butter, and broil over a slow fire; serve in folded napkins.

## NO. 15, STUFFED NO. 1

Bake, then cut off one end and scoop out the inside; season with butter, pepper and salt; beat until light; replace in the skin; close with the piece cut off and put into the oven to heat through. Serve in napkins. Suitable for luncheon.

### NO. 16, STUFFED NO. 2

"Prepare the same as for No. 15, to which add to every pint of potato ¼ pint of minced ham; mix thoroughly, fill the hulls, heat and serve.

### NO. 17, SOUTHERN DISH

Cut cold baked sweet potatoes into slices and put into an earthen dish; add sugar and butter to each layer and bake until slightly brown.

### NO. 18, CROQUETTES

Take two cupfuls of mashed, boiled, steamed or baked sweet potatoes; add the beaten yolks of two eggs and season to taste; stir over the fire until the mass parts from the sides of the pan. When cold, form into small croquettes, roll in egg and bread crumbs, and fry in hot lard to amber color. Serve on napkins.

### NO. 19, SWEET POTATO BALLS

Prepare the same as for croquettes, make into balls and enclose within the center of minced meat.

### NO. 20, PUREE

Take mashed, boiled, steamed or baked sweet potatoes; season and add enough hot milk to moisten; serve like mashed potatoes, or put in pudding dish; dress the top with egg and brown in oven; serve with sauce.

### NO. 21, BROWNED

Cut cold, boiled or stewed sweet potatoes into slices ¼ of an inch thick; add butter, sugar, pepper and salt and put into oven and brown.

## NO. 22, SCALLOPED POTATOES

Wash and peel the potatoes; slice very thin; put in baking dish in layers; season each layer with salt, butter, ½ teacup of sugar, a dash of spice, nutmeg and ginger, cover with milk that has been made ½ cream; bake in moderate oven until tender; serve hot.

## NO. 23, DELICIOUS POTATOES

Wash and pare rather small size potatoes; steam or boil until they can be readily pierced with a fork; dry the surplus water off; have little butter melted in a dish, roll the potatoes in this; place in a quick oven and brown slightly; serve hot.

## NO. 24, HASHED POTATOES

Take cold sweet potatoes, either steamed or boiled, roasted or baked: cut into small pieces, place in a well buttered pan, mince scraps of meat of any kind and stir into it; let brown and serve hot. Chicken makes a most excellent meat to put into it.

## NO. 25, BAKED WITH APPLES

Take four medium sized potatoes and the same number of apples. Wash, peel and cut the potatoes in slices about ¼ of an inch thick; pear and slice the apples in the same way; put in baking dish in alternate layers; sprinkle 1½ cups of sugar over the top, scatter ½ cup of butter also over the top; add 3/4 pint of hot water; bake slowly for one hour; serve steaming hot.

## NO. 26, SWEET POTATO MUFFINS

Boil until thoroughly done, a sweet potato weighing about 3/4 of a pound; mash very fine; pass through a colander to free from lumps; add to it a large tablespoonful of butter and a little salt; whip well; now add ½ cupful of milk and two well beaten eggs, and flour enough to make a soft batter, which will be about two cupfuls. Before adding the flour sift into it one teaspoonful of baking powder. Bake in muffins or gem pans.

## NO. 27, SWEET POTATO PUFFERS

Whip two eggs until quite light; two cups of cold mashed potatoes; one cup of flour into which one teaspoonful of baking powder has been sifted. The potatoes and eggs should be worked together; then the flour and baking powder; roll lightly; cut quickly, and fry in deep fat like doughnuts. Some think a little spice improves the flavor.

## NO. 28, SWEET POTATO SAVORIES

Boil and mash as many sweet potatoes as required; when cold stir in sufficient flour to form into a paste; roll out and cut into small squares, soak a few bread crumbs in water five or ten minutes; squeeze dry; add a little chopped parsley mixed herbs, and a small onion previously soaked in hot water; season with salt and a dash of pepper. Mix all together thoroughly. Put a little on each square or past, and fold over as in sausage rolls; fry in boiling fat till brown; drain and serve.

## NO. 29, SWEET POTATO NUTS

Take one pint of boiled and mashed potatoes, one pint of toasted bread crumbs roll fine, one pint of mixed nut meats chopped fine (peanuts are excellent) season with salt, a little pepper, also sage and mace if desired; take the yolks of two eggs; stir in two teaspoon of baking powder; whip until light; pour into the above mixture and stir well; form into small cakes; dip each into the whites of the eggs, then into shredded cocoanut, and brown in a frying pan containing a little pork fat (not deep fat); turn; brown on both sides.

## NO. 30, SWEET POTATO RICE

Pear and boil the potato in water slightly salted; when done drain off the water, and run through a ricer; server hot with plain or drawn butter. The dry, mealy varieties are especially pleasing when prepared in this way.

## SWEET POTATO FLOUR

There are several grades of this product and quite as many ways to manufacture them. Each one of these flours or meals (as most millers insist upon calling them) has a particular character of its own and is therefore adapted to certain uses the other products are not.

These sweet potato flours are generally speaking of three kinds.

1st. Those made from the uncooked potato.

2nd. Those made from the cooked potato.

3rd. Those made from a careful system of roasting, or from the starch making process. The first two will interest the housewife most, so, therefore, I will dwell almost or quite exclusively on these.

## FLOUR NO. 1, FROM THE RAW POTATO

Here, all that is necessary is to wash, peel, and slice the potatoes real thin, dry in sun, oven or dryer until the pieces are quite brittle, grind very fine in a clean coffee mill, spice mill or any type of mill that will make wheat flour or corn meal; bolt through fine cloth in the same way, as for other flours.

"The fine flour-like particles will pass through, and the coarse granular meal left on the cloths.

## USES

This kind of flour is fine for making mock rye bread, ginger snaps, wafers, waffles, batter cakes, custards, pies, etc. Bread can be made with it, but it makes a dough deficient in elasticity, bread dark in color and a loaf which dries out quickly.

The coarser meals can be cooked in a great variety of ways and make very palatable dishes; they are to be soaked in warm liquid (whatever is desired to cook them in, when soft proceed as for grated potatoes.

## FLOUR NO. 2 FROM COOKED POTATOES

For the making of this flour the potatoes are boiled, or steamed (preferably the later) until done, slice or granulated by making or running through a food chopper and dried until they become very brittle, they are made into flour and meal exactly the same as given for flour No. 1.

## USES

This kind of flour is especially fine for making mock rye bread, cakes, pies, puddings, sauce, gravies, custards, etc.

'Indeed, most people consider a loaf made in the proportion of one-third sweet potato flour to two-thirds wheat flour, superior in flavor and appearance to all wheat flour.

"Many experiments have proved that either the mashed sweet potato or the sweet potato flour may be used in bread up to as high as 50%, but at this point it becomes decidedly potato-like in texture and flavor but not unpalatable or unwholesome.

## FLOUR NO. 3 FROM PULP

This flour is made from the pulp after the starch has been removed, it is dried without cooking, ground and bolted exactly the same as recommended for the other flours."

"When made into puddings, pies, blanc-mange, etc., the same as shredded cocoanut, it resembles it very much in taste and texture and is very palatable, and is a most welcome addition to the dietary.

"It can also be used in the making of bread and is especially valuable where people object to a loaf with the least bit of sweet taste, also where they wish one with as little starch and sugar as possible.

## SWEET POTATO STARCH

This is very easily made, all that is necessary is to grate the potato, the finer the better, put into a cheese cloth or thin muslin bag and dip up and down, in a vessel of water, squeezing occasionally, continue washing as long as the washings are very milky.

Allow it to settle five or six hours or until the water becomes clear, pour off; rewash the starch, which will be in the bottom of the vessel, stir up well, allow to settle again, pour off the water and let dry, keep the same as an ordinary starch.

## USES

Use exactly the same as corn starch in cooking; I am confident you will find it superior to corn starch; it makes a very fine quality of library paste, and has very powerful adhesive qualities.

"In certain parts and trades it is almost indispensable.

## SWEET POTATO BISCUITS

- Take:
- ½ cupful mashed sweet potatoes,

- 1 cupful flour,
- 4 teaspoons baking powder,
- ½ tablespoon salt,
- 2 tablespoons butter or lard.

Milk sufficient to make a soft dough. Sift the flour, salt, and baking powder together several times; add these to the potatoes, mixing in with a knife.

## SWEET POTATO SUGAR

By saving the water in which the pulp was washed first, in the starch making process, and boiling down, the same as for any syrup, a very palatable, non crystaline sugar will be the result; this sugar or syrup can be used in many ways.

Here in the South and other sections of the country where fresh potatoes can be had almost or quite the year round, the flour is not a necessity for bread making; but for commercial purposes there are almost unlimited possibilities, and is destined to become more popular as fast as the public finds out what a delicious, appetizing and wholesome product these flours are.

Our method of using follows with the hope that thousands of house-wives will try out this most satisfactory way to conserve wheat flour.

## HOUSEHOLD RECIPES

## SWEET POTATO BREAD

- Take:
- 1 cup finely mashed sweet potatoes,
- 2 tablespoons warm water,
- ½ yeast cake,
- 1 teaspoon salt,

Two and 3/4 cups flour, or sufficient to make a soft dough.

Add the salt to the potatoes, and the yeast; put in the water; add flour enough to make a smooth sponge (about a cupful); cover, and set in a warm place to rise.

When light add the remainder of the flour or whatever is needed to make a smooth, elastic dough. Cover, and let rise until light; mould; shape into loaves or rolls; let rise and bake.

Many variations of the above bread can be made by adding sugar, butter, lard, nuts, spices, etc.

## SWEET POTATO BISCUITS NO. 1

Now work the fat into the mixture lightly; add the milk; work quickly and lightly until a soft dough is formed; turn out on a floured board; pat and roll out lightly until about one-half inch thick; cut into biscuits; place on buttered or greased pans, and bake twelve or fifteen minutes in a quick oven.

## SWEET POTATO BISCUITS NO. 2 (EXTRA FINE)

Take:

- 1 cup boiled and finely mashed sweet potatoes,
- 2 eggs, well beaten,
- 2 cups flour,
- 2 teaspoons baking powder, Page 125
- 1 teaspoon salt,
- 2 scant tablespoons melted butter or lard,
- 1 tablespoon sugar, (if desired),
- 2 cups milk.

Mix together all the dry ingredients, and stir into the milk, beaten eggs and potato."

"If too soft add more flour, sufficient to make a soft dough. Roll out lightly; cut with a biscuit cutter; bake in quick oven.

SWEET POTATO BREAD (baker's method)

This recipe was given to me by Mr. J. M. Colter, who has charge of the Institute's Bakery:

Take:

79 pounds of wheat flour; 30 pounds of finely mashed sweet potatoes; 40 pounds of water; 1½ pounds of salt; 1 pound of sugar; 1 pound of lard; 8 pounds of compress yeast.

Every other operation is exactly the same as for bread or rolls made from all wheat flour.

Mr. W. T. Shehee, Steward of Boarding Department, says it not only gives universal satisfaction, but is preferred by many to bread or rolls made from all wheat flour.

In making up these dietaries the central thought has been to give the maximum amount of nourishment at the minimum cost.

As a rule we are wasteful; we do not know how to save. Ignorance in the kitchen is one of the worst curses that ever afflicted humanity, and is directly or indirectly responsible for more deaths than all the armies combined. It sacrifices human life from the following angles:

1. A poor selection of food; that is, foodstuff lacking in the constituents necessary to build up the body and keep healthy.

2. Bad combinations of food; that is, there are many foodstuffs good within themselves, but when combined with other material creates an un-natural appetite; and quite frequently the body is un-

nourished, unduly stimulated, and as a result often leads to strong drink, bad morals, and bad manners.

3. Bad preparation of food. In this I think I make a conservative statement when I say that 75 per cent of those who are entrusted with this important charge are deficient. Here is the very hot-bed for indigestion, constipation, sour stomach, mal-nutrition, colic, and a host of other stomach troubles.

# CHAPTER XIII.

## HOW TO MAKE AND SAVE MONEY ON THE FARM

It is highly important that every farmer and his family look ahead, plan and work together with all their might to raise and save every possible thing on the farm, garden, orchard, etc., that can be used as food for either man or beast.

The making and saving money on the farm depends almost wholly upon the careful study and heed given to the following questions:

QUESTION 1  Should the farmer keep a cow?
ANSWER Yes, every farmer should keep one or two good cows; a good cow is half of any family's living, as she will furnish all the butter, milk, cream, etc., that the ordinary family can use, and if properly cared for a surplus can be had to sell. There are a number of foods that are more palatable, more healthy, and more economical when seasoned with milk and butter than when seasoned with lard or any other kind of shortening. Good bread, rich milk, and nice butter furnish almost a completely balanced ration.

QUESTION 2    "Should a farmer raise chickens?
ANSWER      Yes, by all means every farmer should start with twelve good hens and one rooster. With a little care they will furnish all the eggs needed in the family, some meat, and a surplus at times to exchange for clothing and other necessities. Page 128 A few guineas, ducks, turkeys, and a pair or two of geese will bring you much pleasure and profit at practically no cash outlay.

QUESTION 3
Should a farmer have a garden?
ANSWER

Yes, nothing will pay him better. It is one of the greatest money-makers on the farm. It makes money in two principal ways.

(a) It furnishes a great variety of food stuff, which is absolutely essential to good health and the proper strength of both mind and body. If we eat plenty of good food, well cooked vegetables every day, all other things being equal, we can do more work and better work than if we did not. We shall not get so tired, weary, and have to consult the doctor so often, and pay out such heavy doctor bills.

(b) In the garden there should be always a surplus of something to sell, especially of beans, peas, melons, onions, white and sweet potatoes, tomatoes, cabbage, turnips, rutabagas, rape, pumpkins, beets, squash, etc. The garden should furnish many things for canning, pickling, and preserving. The opening of the drying, canning, and preserving season for fruits and vegetables begins here.

Every year it is painfully apparent that fully two-thirds of our fruits and tons of vegetables go to waste. These, with a little effort in the direction of canning, preserving and drying can be converted into nutritious and palatable dainties, sufficient to last throughout the winter and spring months.

PREPARATION   An ordinary iron or tin wash boiler, with a heavy wire or slatted bottom, will answer the purpose for cooking. Thoroughly clean the jars; fill; place them in the cooker so that they will not touch each other; pour three or four inches of water in the cooker; put on the cover and steam (let boil), Page 129 briskly the length of time necessary for the particular fruit or vegetable you are canning.

METHODS CORN   Shear off the grains with a sharp knife; pack the jars or cans full; salt to taste; fill them up to the top with cold water; put on the rubber rings, and screw on the tops loosely; keep the water boiling for one hour; remove the cover of the boiler and screw down the caps. On the second day loosen the caps, and boil again for one hour. Seal again, and repeat the same the third day. They may now be permanently sealed and placed in a cool, dark, dry place.    Thoroughly cook the fruit or vegetable in a granite or porcelain-linked kettle; remove the cans or jars from the boiling water; fill and seal at once. They often keep admirably in this way, but the flavor is never so fine or the appearance so attractive.

STRING BEANS    String, top, and tail exactly as for cooking; pack tightly whole or jars or cans, and treat the same as for corn.

OKRA    (Use only tender Okra)    Wash in cold water; cut off the steams and tips; leave whole or jars or cans and treat the same as for corn.

ENGLISH PEAS AND LIMA BEANS    Shell; wash in cold water, and treat the same as for corn. (Follow the same process for lima beans).

EGG PLANT    Peel and cut into cubes, or slices about an inch thick; Page 130 drop in boiling water for fifteen or twenty minutes, pack in jars or cans, and treat the same as for corn.
ASPARAGUS    Take the nice, tender tips; wash in cold water, and treat the same as for corn. PARSNIPS,
CARROTS, PUMPKINS, AND SQUASH    Wash, peel, and grate; slice or cut in dice (squares); fill the cans and treat the same as for corn.

TOMATOES    Take nice, ripe tomatoes; dip them in boiling water for a few minutes; immediatly plunge into cold water; remove the skins; fill the cans, and treat the same as for corn. Two tablespoons of sugar to the half-gallon will improve the flavor.

BEETS    Wash young, tender beets; prepare the same as for cooking; cook until done; remove the skins; cut in thin slices, pack into the jars and treat the same as for corn. If a pickle is desired, mix equal parts of good vinegar and water, sweeten to taste, and cover the beets with this mixture instead of water. (Use only glass jars where vinegar is used).

SAUERKRAUT    Take a clean keg, barrel, or jar; select good, firm cabbage heads; remove the outer leaves; wash and quarter as for cooking; shred with a spade, sharp knife, or slaw cutter until very fine; rub the sides and bottom of the vessel with salt; put in a two or three inch layer of shredded cabbage; pound down with a wood pestle; another layer of cabbage and salt, pounding as before; continue this process until the vessel is as full as you desire; cover over with cabbage leaves, and weight down with a heavy stone weight; make a weak brine of salt and water, and cover the cabbage; use just a trifle more salt Page 131 than for cooking; tie a thin cloth over the vessel to keep out worms, put in a cool, dry place.

SWEET POTATOES    Select medium-sized potatoes; boil until two-thirds done; scrape off the skins; cut (if too large for the cans) into thick slices or strips; pack in the jars or cans tightly; cover with a thin syrup of water and sugar (one and one-half pounds of sugar to one gallon of water); treat afterwards exactly as for corn.

BLACKBERRIES    In all cases where cans or jars are used they are to be thoroughly cleaned. Use twelve quarts blackberries, two quarts sugar; pack tightly in jars, and cook the same as for corn.

HUCKLEBERRIES    Take twelve quarts of berries; one quart sugar; one pint water; put water, berries and sugar in the preserving kettle; heat slowly; boil fifteen minutes, counting from the time contents of the kettle began to bubble (boil); pour in hot jars, and seal at once.

GRAPES, MUSCADINES, SCUPPERNONGS    Take six quarts of grapes, one quart sugar, one gill water; squeeze the pulp of the grapes out of the skins; cook the pulp five minutes, and then rub through a sieve fine enough to hold back the seeds; put the water, skins and pulp into the preserving kettle, and heat slowly to the boiling point; skin the fruit and add the sugar; boil five minutes; pour into hot jars, and seal.

PEACHES     Take eight quarts peaches, one quart sugar, three quarts Page 132 water; put the sugar and water together; boil and skim; pare the peaches; cut in halves; remove the stones unless you wish them whole; put in the preserving kettle; cover with the hot syrup; gently boil fifteen minutes skimming carefully; place the peaches in hot jars; cover with the syrup, and seal.   Treat plums the same as peaches, but double the quantity of sugar. The skins and seeds need not be removed.

STRAWBERRIES    Can the same as for blackberries; skim out the berries; put in hot jars; boil down the syrup thick and pour it over them; seal and set in a cool place.

PEARS AND APPLES    Treat exactly the same as for peaches; if they are hard, boil until tender.  In canning fruit no sugar is needed at all, but it makes a much choicer product where it is used.

 HOW TO DRY FRUITS AND VEGETABLES      Drying is without doubt the simplest and best method of preserving a number of fruits and vegetables. And it is a source of much regret that such a few know how to appreciate the delicious taste of home dried fruits and vegetables. "The fruits and vegetables listed on the following pages are more or less abundant throughout the South, and the methods given show how easily and how cheaply they may be taken care of.

FURNACES FOR DRYING      There are several inexpensive and satisfactory furnaces for the rapid drying of fruits and vegetables, which any farmer can make. One of the simplest is a furnace made just like one for making syrup. Cover with a heavy piece of sheet iron; cover this three or four inches deep with clean sand; put on a very open slatted cover just above it. The Page 133 fruits or vegetables to be dried may be placed in separate slatted trays and one set above the other, if suitable frame work is made so they may be pushed in and pulled out, like bureau drawers.      If the sides are walled up with brick or tin so as to keep in the heat, the drying will be very fast. Several small openings should be left in the sides to carry off the moist air. A bushel or more of fruit or vegetables may be dried at one time in this way.

FRUITS   Begin drying just as soon as the seed matures, or as soon as the fruit is two-thirds ripe, and continue as long as you can handle it without mashing to a pulp.   Caution, in drying either fruits, or vegetables in the sun screen wire or mosquito netting should be stretched over a suitable frame to keep off the flies and other insects and everything, of course, must be scrupulously clean if a superior flavored, the most attractive appearing and the most appetizing, healthy and wholesome product is desired.

STRAWBERRY LEATHER (Delicious)   Take thoroughly ripe strawberries; mash to a pulp; spread on platters, and dry in the sun or oven; when dry, dust with powdered sugar, and roll up like a jelly cake, cut into suitable sized pieces and pack away in water and use for pies, short cake, sauce, tarts, etc. The powdered sugar is a matter of taste and may be left off if desired.

PEACH LEATHER (Extra good)   Select over ripe peaches and make exactly as recommended for strawberry leather.

FIG LEATHER NO. 1   Make exactly the same as for strawberries.

FIG LEATHER NO. 2 (Delicious)   Mix one-half peaches and one-half figs and proceed the same as for strawberries.
"NOTE: The above method of making leathers applies to almost any kind of soft, pulpy fruit.

DRIED STRAWBERRIES   Put the berries in a moderate oven, heat through thoroughly, but not enough to become soft and juicy, spread out in the sun for finish in the oven.

BLACKBERRIES AND DEWBERRIES   Treat exactly the same as recommended for strawberries.

NOTE: If a seedless product is desired, this may be done by pressing the pulp through a fine sieve before drying.

PLUMS DRIED PLUMS NO. 1   Select medium ripe plums, cover with boiling water, cover the vessel and let stand twenty minutes; drain and spread in the sun to dry. Stir occasionally; when dry examine them frequently and at the first appearance of worms put in the oven and heat for a few minutes. In cooking, soak in cold water for a few hours the same as for other dried fruit.

DRIED PLUMS NO. 2   After peeling the plums, allow half pound of sugar to one pound of fruit. Put fruit and sugar in layers in a preserving kettle. Heat slowly until the sugar is dissolved, then boil until clear. Spread the fruit on platters in the sun and turn over until quite dry. Pack in layers with sugar in stone or glass jars. Plums that are dried in this way are extra fine.

FIGS   There are a number of ways to dry figs, some of them quite complex. I am giving only methods suitable for the home. "Take well ripened figs (but not mushy), treat the same as for strawberries, cut into halves and finish in the sun or oven. Frequent dusting with powdered sugar during the drying process makes a delicious confection.

PEACHES   Take ripe, firm peaches, peel, cut from the seed if cling stones, break open if free stones. Quarter or cut slices, spread in the sun or dry in the oven. The peelings may be left on if desired; the product of course is not so fine.

OKRA   Steam until two-thirds done; split in quarters the thickest pods, and dry the same as corn.

PEARS   Peel, core, slice and dry the same as recommended for peaches.

APPLES   Peel, core, quarter or slice and dry the same as recommended for peaches.

GRAPES, MUSCADINES (Delicious)   Gather when ripe, wash, put in a porcelain or granite preserving kettle, cover with boiling water, let simmer until the berries are hot through and the hulls have turned a reddish color, now stir in a scant tablespoon of baking soda to the gallon of fruit; drain off this water, wash in three more waters, being careful each time not to mash the berries. They Page 136 may now be dried whole or made into a leather the same as recommended for strawberries. I much prefer the leather, the hulls will be very tender and the fruit a fine flavor. The seed smay be removed by pressing through a colander. I wish every housewife would try this.

CULTIVATED GRAPES   All cultivated grapes may be dried in the same way, except the soda should be omitted in the process.

CORN   Corn is delicious when dried. Take tender roasting ears; steam until nearly done; cut from the cob with a sharp knife; spread thinly upon boards or dishes; put in the sun to dry. If the tops of the grains are shaved off and the pulp scraped out, leaving most of the bran on the cob, it makes a much finer product. In cooking, it should be soaked for an hour or two in cold water before the final cooking.

PUMPKIN   Peel and cut discs about an inch thick or in thin slices; spread in the sun to dry; soak several hours in cold water before cooking.

STRING BEANS   Select very young, tender beans, wash and cut off both stem and blossom ends. Cut into one-inch lengths, steam until about one-fourth done or until they lose their green appearance. Spread on trays and dry as any other fruit or vegetable. Soak for several hours in cold water before cooking.

HOW TO DRY TOMATOES   If it were generally known what a distinct and delicious product the tomato makes when properly dried, I am sure every housewife would dry a few pounds. When eaten as a confection it is far superior to many of the so-called choice candies sold at fancy prices.

METHOD NO. 1     Take thoroughly ripe tomatoes; wash and slice or chop; put in preserving kettle, and cook slowly until thoroughly done; pass through a colander to remove the skins and hard cores; return to the kettle and boil until thick like jam; spread on plates, and dry in the sun or oven. When dry roll up like jelly-cake, or cut into squares and put away the same as any other dried fruit or vegetable.     When wanted for use soak in a little cold water until soft, then use exactly the same as tomato paste.     Delicious catsup can be made from this dried paste by softening and adding the required amount of vinegar and spices.

METHOD NO. 2
Select tomatoes that are full-grown but green, or just beginning to tinge with color. Treat in every way exactly the same as for Method No. 1.

This paste will be pleasingly tart, and is especially fine for making green tomato pies, which is an old family favorite among pies.     We hope that every housewife will try one or both of these methods.

INSECTS
In this climate insects are very troublesome to dried fruit or vegetables. I have had excellent success by putting the dried fruit or vegetables in the oven and heating them real hot, sufficiently to kill any lurking insects or their eggs; then pouring them into clean paper bags, tying the mouth tightly and suspending the bags, not a single insect was ever found in the bags, although they were kept several months.

JELLIES
Put the fruit in a stone jar placed in a boiler of hot water. When fruit is sufficiently softened, strain through a thin muslin bag; place juice in a preserving kettle, and allow one pound of sugar to a pint of juice (one and one-eighth of a pound if the juice is very sour). While heating juice, place the sugar in a dish in the oven; allow juice to boil twenty minutes; add heated sugar; let all come to a boil and remove

from the fire; having scalded glasses, pour them brim full and allow to stand in the sun for a day or until the jelly is thoroughly set; cover with melted paraffin or with tissue paper, saturated with brandy.

PICKLES

Cucumbers, small, green cantaloupes, citron, watermelon rinds, green beans, cabbage, green tomatoes, etc., may be packed down in brine (salt water) made strong enough to float an egg; pack tightly in wooden or stone vessels. When desired for pickles soak in cold water until all the salt is out, and proceed in the usual manner for sweet, sour or spiced pickle.

QUESTION 4
Should a farmer try to raise fruit?

ANSWER
Yes, fruit is an absolute necessity in the diet. No person can remain strong and vigorous in mind and body very long who neglects to make fruits of some kind a part of the daily diet. Every farmer should have a few peach, pear, plum, fig, and apple trees on his place, also grape vines, strawberries, etc. A few trees and bushes well cared for will furnish sufficient fruit for the needs of the family. Nut trees such as pecan, walnuts, chestnuts, hickory nuts, etc., are fine shade trees, and the nuts are becoming more and more a part of the diet, taking the place of meat

QUESTION 5
Should a farmer raise hogs?

ANSWER
Yes, for the following reasons:

(a) No other animal converts into meat so much foodstuff that would otherwise go to waste.

(b) They will furnish us all of our meat, lard and the many other choice dainties that no meat is so popular in supplying.

(c) There is a great demand for hogs at all times; the demand is always greater than the supply. They are sure mortgage lifters, and will pay any farmer out of debt if he will give them a chance.

(d) Hogs are easily raised; they will eat and thrive on weeds, nuts, and fruits of most any kind. These, however, are especially good: wild primrose, smooth and thorny careless weeds (pig weeds), purslane (persley), wild plums, acorns, beechnuts, nut grass, etc.

The following choice foods can be easily grown; sweet potatoes, sorghum millet, corn, peanuts, velvet beans, rape, collards, cabbage, turnips, beets, pumpkins, cow peas, soja, Bermuda grass; also wheat, rye, oats, hurr and crimson clover, etc., for winter pasture.

QUESTION 6   Should a farmer try to raise stock? ANSWER   Yes, every bit that he possibly can. In addition to hogs and poultry, he should have mares that would bring colts every year. With proper care they will do all the farm work and raise the colts too. A few sheep, goats, or an extra cow or two will turn a great deal of roughage into meat, and at the same time make much valuable fertilizer for the land.

QUESTION 7     What shall we do for fertilizer? Some farmers are actually too poor to buy sufficient quantities of the commercial mixtures.
ANSWER
There are many thousands of tons of the finest fertilizers going to waste all over the South, in the form of decaying leaves of the forest and the rich sediment of the swamp, known as muck. Every idle moment from now until planting time should be put in gathering up these fertilizers. Make the mixtures (compost) as follows:

(a) Build pen to hold as much as you wish.

(b) Spread two wagon-loads of muck and leaves over the bottom of the pen; then one load of barnyard manure; build up in this way until the pen is full.

(c) Put a rough shed over it sufficient to turn the bulk of water from heavy rains or mound up like a potato hill. This is to prevent the excess of water from washing out the fertilizer constituents.

(d) Put into this compost-heap all the wood ashes, old plaster, waste lime, rags, paper, or any matter that will decay quickly. Bones beaten up fine are also excellent. If you cannot get the barnyard manure make the compost without it. You will be agreeably surprised at the increased yield of crops of all kinds.

(c) Break land deep (eight to nine inches) and thoroughly; lay off rows with a middle-burster or two-horse plow; put compost in drills at the rate of twenty tons to the acre on medium land, and twenty-five tons to the acre on very poor land; plant directly on the fertilizer; cultivate in the usual manner.

QUESTION 8   What shall I do with the Boll Weevil? In all probability it is here to stay.

ANSWER   Yes, the weevil is here and will likely stay, but extensive experiments prove that it may be controlled as follows:

(a) Prepare all land good and deep with a two-horse plow.

(b) Fertilize well.

(c) Plant an early variety of seed.

(d) Stir the ground often to keep the cotton growing.

(e) Follow only approved methods of fighting the boll weevil. Write to the director of your own State Experiment Station for bulletins on the growing of cotton they will be glad to send the results of their latest findings. Read and follow the suggestions with care.

(f) Pick as fast as it opens.

(g) When through gathering the bottom and middle crops, destroy the stalks at once, and sow the field in a grain crop, such as oats, rye, wheat, barley, etc., and if for hay only, mix one-fourth of hairy vetch seed to three-fourths of any one of the above grains.

(h) Clean off and burn all the rubbish from ditch banks, fence corners, and waste places, as the old weevils hide in these places and winter over.

(i) Encourage your neighbors to do the same. In this way the weevil will be reduced to starvation; so much so that the problem of control will be easy.

QUESTION 9    Since the coming of the boll weevil, what is the farmer going to do for a money crop?

ANSWER   'There are several crops, if wisely handled, from which the farmer can realize more money than from cotton; viz., corn, velvet beans, peanuts, sweet potatoes, and cow peas. If a paying market cannot be had for the raw product, they should be fed to stock, and turned into milk, meat, butter, eggs, lard, etc. There are but few, if any, better stock-raising countries than ours. If the manure from these animals is carefully saved and returned to the land, practically all of our fertilizer questions will be settled and our land will respond almost or quite equal to virgin soil.

QUESTION 10
Would a renter or share-cropper attempt to carry out the above suggestions?

ANSWER
Yes, just as far as possible; he should set out trees, clean off ditch banks, make such repairs as he can, and in every way strive to leave the place in better condition than when he took possession. It will mean money in your pockets, aside from the great value of forming correct habits of living.

QUESTION 11
Will it pay a farmer to take an agricultural paper?

ANSWER
Yes, it necessary. He should not only take one or two good agricultural papers, but others as well. He must study markets, crops, weather, supply and demand, and a host of other things which affects him and his business. It is just as important to the farmer as to the merchant. In fact, it is the only way that either can keep abreast of the times.

QUESTION 12    Should the farmer attempt to have a pretty dooryard with flowers?

ANSWER    Yes, by all means, for the reasons which follow:

(a) They are another form of God's silent messengers, and the 'sweetest thing he ever made and forgot to put a soul into.'

(b) We often send for the doctor and take a lot of strong, disagreeable medicine when all we need is a bunch of beautiful flowers from loving hands.

(c) They are soothing and restful to the tired body and brains.

(d) A love for flowers denotes refinement and culture.

(e) Pretty door yards and charming surroundings increase the value of property, and encourage the very best class of people to become our neighbors.

ADDITIONAL WAYS TO MAKE MONEY

(1) There is always a demand for early cabbage, tomatoes, sweet potatoes, peppers, and egg plants. All of these are easily grown in hot-beds, cold frames, or in boxes in sunny windows.

(2) Lettuce, parsley, radishes, and onions, are easily grown in the same way as above described, and at this time of the year sell readily.

(3) Light wood from fat pine trees and stumps sell readily, as well as good dry wood. In many places there are large quantities of old dead trees going to waste that would make excellent wood and kindling, which would sell without any trouble if cut and brought to market. A few hours a week spent in this way will bring surprising returns.

(4) Homemade shingles, fence palings, rustic chairs, settees, tables, baskets, horse collars, quilts, rugs, shuck mats, axe, hatchet, hoe and fork handles can be sold if made well, and a reasonable price asked for them. The same is true with the many styles of homemade lace, embroidery and other kinds of fancy work.

(5) Nearly every one prefers home-canned and home-preserved fruits and vegetables to those put up in a commercial way, and anyone doing this artistically and cheaply would command patronage.
(6) Choice lye hominy is always in demand, and to the eneregtic a nice trade can be worked up in almost any town or thickly settled community.

LYE HOMINY  Here is a dish that is not only nourishing, but relished universally by almost everyone during the winter and spring months, and should appear on the table in some tempting way at least three or four times a week. Recipe: Select sound, white corn; to every gallon of corn use one tablespoon of concentrated lye. Cover the corn with water; boil slowly until the skin comes off easily and the dark tips on the grains near the eye begin to come out; pour into a vessel and wash thoroughly; let soak (preferably overnight) in plenty of cold water; drain; return to kettle, and boil in plenty of water until tender; put in a stone jar and set in a cool place, and it will keep several days. One-half gallon of hardwood ashes put in a sack and boiled with the corn will answer the same purpose, except it is not so quick a method.

(7) Walnuts, hickory nuts, pecan, beechnuts and peanuts make delicious candies and nut cakes, which always find a ready sale when attractively put upon the market.

(8) Choice lettuce, parsley, radishes, onions, etc., are easily grown in winter, and find ready sale at good prices.

(9) Have one or two hogs extra. They can be raised, beginning in April with pigs, to maturity with practically no cash outlay, by giving them all the slop and refuse vegetables from the garden, plus the weeds, etc., that grow in such abundance everywhere. Home-made sausage is a luxury, and all one has to do is to let people know one has it to sell. The demand here is never satisfied. Much the same is true of souse, hog's-head cheese, scrapel, pigs feet and ears, chitterlings, together with a fine lot of choice lard and cracklings.

(10) "Choice, well cured hay finds a ready market. The following grasses, fodders, etc., should be cut, dried, and made secure before the frost falls on them. Pea vines, crab grass, water grass, late patches of corn, sorghum, Johnson grass, ribbon cane blades and tops for the cow, sweet potato vines, velvet beans, soja beans, etc. These are only a few of the many ways of becoming thrifty and self-supporting. Begin at once to put some of them into effect."

# CHAPTER XIV.
# HOW TO RAISE PIGS WITH LITTLE MONEY

But few people realize how much money there is in hogs, how quickly and easily they can be raised with but little or no outlay.

ADVANTAGES First--"Nature has been lavish in providing a number of superior foodstuffs, some one or more of which may be had simply for the gathering. Second--"Nearly every kind of temperate and sub-tropical foodstuffs can be grown easily, and some of them preserved for feeding the year round. Third--"The climate is practically perfect.

Fourth--"An abundance of clean, fresh, wholesome water can be had at all times. Fifth--"Much of the soil is sandy, well-drained, and ideal for hog raising.

Six--"There is always a good market for choice pork and pork products. Seventh--"No farm animals multiply as fast as hogs except chicken. Eight--"Hogs are great scavengers, converting into meat much of the waste from kitchen, farm, garden, orchard, dairy, etc. Ninth--"The losses from cholera here in Macon County are exceedingly small, and can yet be reduced if the proper precautions are taken. Tenth--"Hog raising is the most fitting complement to the boys' corn clubs and girls' canning clubs, as both of these movements should furnish large quantities of cheap pork-producing foods.

HOW TO BEGIN
Choose first a good bread. Of the many good types, the Berkshire, Essex, and Poland China seem to be the most popular here in the South; in fact, the Berkshires are my choice. Select two female pigs of good breeding if you are able to pay for them; if not, strong, healthy ones--mongrels, or any sort obtainable. Breed only to good, well-bred male, never to a scrub. These sows, with proper care, will

give you two litters of pigs per year, and at each farrowing time will drop six to ten fine, healthy little porkers. The above picture is a small sketch of the swine-herd, at Tuskegee Institute. The pigs are grazing on a vegetable crop, which illustrates one of the many ways of raising thorough-bred hogs with little money.

# CHAPTER XV.
# HOUSING

In a climate as mild as this, expensive houses are unnecessary. A small lean-to (shed) house, 6×6 feet or 8×8, just high enough in the back to clear the head, and tall enough in front to form a good water-shed, is quite sufficient. The top may be covered with boards, shingles, straw, grass, or anything that is the cheapest and easiest to obtain.

FEEDING How to secure food for one, two, or several hogs presents an insurmountable problem to many, when in truth and in fact, Macon County as well as many other sections of the South, is usually blessed with an abundance of just the kinds of foods for the production of the choicest pork and pork products in the world. For the sake of clearness I am dividing the foodstuffs into two divisions as follows:

1--NATIVE FOODS

WILD PRIMROSE--A plant bearing a slight resemblance to lettuce when young. It bears yellow flowers and forms an almost round mat on the ground from two to three feet in diameter in rich soil. An analysis of this plant shows it to be highly nutritious, and hogs eat it greedily and thrive off it. In this locality it is large enough to begin pulling and feeding by the last of February. SMOOTH AND

THORNY CARELESS WEEDS (Pig-weeds)--Come in abundance in April and May. These weeds are very rich in food material and hogs are very fond of them.

WILD PLUMS--Are usually abundant from the latter part of May to August. Their value as a hog-food is too well known to need discussion here.

ACORNS--Of all kinds, usually abundant in September, October, November, and December are well known and recognized in the feeding for choice pork.

BEECH NUTS--Are often plentiful in October, November and December. Nothing produces finer bacon than such nuts.

NUT GRASS--This plant is the wild chufa, and has almost as high a feeding value as the cultivated chufa. If you have a sufficient amount of nut-infested ground, divide it up into plats and let the hogs root the nuts out; when one plat has been thoroughly rooted overturn them in upon another.

PURSLANE (Pusley)--Appears in May, June and July and is among the best of the pigweeds for feeding swine.

2--FOODS THAT CAN BE GROWN

SWEET POTATOES--Should head the list, as they can be so easily grown and possess almost as high a fattening value as corn in the production of pork. The Cuban Queen, and Red Nansemond should be grown for this purpose. These two are selected on account of their large yield, but any variety will do.

SORGHUM MILLET--Plant a few rows about the middle of March solely for the hogs. Cut a little bunch and give them every day just as soon as it is large enough.

CORN--Its feeding value is too well known to need any discussion here.

PEANUTS--In this we have practically a perfect food. Two crops a year of the Spanish variety can be grown. Plant the first crop by the 15th of April--they will be fully matured by the middle of July. Dig, plow up the ground, and plant it again.

RAPE, COLLARDS, CABBAGE, TURNIPS, BEETS--All sorts of garden vegetables, hogs will eat with a relish. They are especially fond of watermelons and cantaloupes.

PUMPKINS--"Either cooked or raw, make a superior food for hogs. The same is true of cashews, squash, etc.

COW PEAS--"Hogs are very fond of grazing on green cow peas, and seem to thrive almost if not as well as on clover pasture, Soja beans are also very fine.

BERMUDA GRASS-- A good Bermuda-grass pasture is almost synonymous to an abundance of choice, cheap pork if properly grazed by the hogs. Wheat, rye and oats, Burr and crimson clover make an excellent winter pasture if sown early.

THINGS TO BEAR IN MIND   1. That the health and success of pig raising depends largely upon keeping the quarters where the pigs stay, clean--the houses should never be allowed to become filthy. Clean out every few days, and keep well whitewashed.

2. Keep the following mixture where they can get it at all times:

To one peck of charcoal broken into small pieces, mix-- 1 pint salt 1 pint flowers of sulphur (powdered sulphur) 1 pint copperas. This is a fine tonic as well as a cleanser of intestinal impurities.

3. Feed liberally, but change the diet often. Cook the food at times. Never allow them to suffer for clean, fresh water.

4. Remember, it is dangerous to feed swill that has lye, soap, washing powders, glass, etc., in it.  5. Skim milk or milk or any kind is excellent for hogs of all ages, but especially fine for growing pigs."

POULTRY RAISING

Of all the get-rich-quick schemes there is probably none more productive of delusion than that of poultry raising on paper. And yet, with the proper facilities and applied intelligence, possibly more handsome returns can be had from poultry than any other industry in proportion to the amount of capital invested and the readiness with which results can be obtained.

There is an idea prevalent that poultry cannot be successfully raised in the South. This saying has been so often repeated and the apparent truth so universally verified that Page 150 the majority of our people believe it and make but little or no effort to prove it false.

Years of costly experimentation and investigation have removed many of the apparent insurmountable obstacles, so that there remains no doubt as to its possibilities. It is therefore the purpose of this chapter to set forth, in as clear and concise a way as possible, a number of rules and suggestions which, if carried out, will enable an amateur to successfully grapple with this problem.

NATURAL ADVANTAGES
In our investigations the following truths were brought to light:
(a). That the country as a whole is high, well drained, with mild climate, plenty of good sharp sand, and that throughout the county green stuff of some sort, such as wheat, oats, rye, clover, vetch, rape, etc., may be grown the year round. Good, wholesome water is also plentiful. All the above are indispensable adjuncts to successful poultry raising.

MARKETS
I think I am safe in the assertion that, as far back as history records, there never was a time without a good market for poultry and poultry products. In fact, in recent years the demand has been far in excess of the supply.

Should production go beyond home demands, we are very near three great centers of consumption, Montgomery, Birmingham and

Atlanta, and in addition to these we have the most excellent facilities for reaching all the points north, south, east and west.

(b). We found further that the fowl almost without exception throughout the county, was of a very poor class of mongrels (mixed breeds), which showed to a marked degree the weakening effect of inbreeding and poor selection or no selection at all.

(c). That these weak, anemic fowls were subject to all kinds of diseases as they sickened and died in large numbers under the most favorable treatment we could give them. (d). That they were very poor layers; that the eggs produced were low in fertility and often sterile altogether; that the chicks from the eggs that did hatch were weak and but few able to stand artificial conditions, so an exceedingly small number ever reached markable size.

ORIGIN AND BUILDING UP OF THE FLOCK
Before we can intelligently build up a flock we must of necessity know something of the origin of the various birds with which we must deal. The best authorities claim that all our splendid varieties, types and assortment of fowl originated from a jungle fowl of India. This wild chicken was quite small, and in color, resembled our black breasted game breed. The Prairie chicken and the quail belong to the same zoological family and all have strikingly similar habits.

"There is but little doubt that the chicken spread from its natural home in India, east and west, until its origin was almost lost by reason of its large and variable numbers and wide distribution.

Out of the eighty-seven standards and a large number of promiscuous varieties of chickens raised in this country, I shall deal with only a few that have proved the best by actual test.

Professor George E. Howard, in eminent authority on poultry has subdivided the ten great classes into which the various breeds of poultry are divided, and reduced them to four.

THE AMERICAN CLASS
The Barred, Buff, Pea Comb Barred and White Plymouth Rocks; Silver, Golden, White, Buff and Black Wyandottes; Black, Mottled and White Javas; American Dominiques and Jersey.

BLUES--All are the most conspicuous members of this group. They are reasonably good layers, make excellent mothers and turn out a nice lot of meat when killed.

BARRED PLYMOUTH ROCK
With us this is the most popular of all the above breeds, being good layers, reasonably free from disease, fine mothers, and easy to keep. Their history dates back over a quarter of a century, being constantly improved from year to year until almost a perfect fowl has been produced. They are of good size, full-grown cock often weighing as much as 9½ pounds, and hens 7½ pounds. The meat is of superior quality.

MEDITERRANEAN CLASS
The Brown, Rose Comb Brown, White, Rose Comb White, Black, Dominique, Buff and Silver Duckwing Leghorns, Black and White Minorcas, Andalusians, and Black Spanish, all belong to the above class and are noted for their great egg production. Aside from this they have but little to recommend them, as they are too small for market purposes, cannot relied upon as mothers, are high-flyers, and hard to keep just where wanted.

WHITE AND BROWN LEGHORNS
These are the best known and the best established of all the bereds. Fancy must dictate which of the breeds you will choose, as there are practically no points of superiority in them except the color. They are highly organized, nervous egg machines, and if warmly housed, and properly fed, are the best of all winter layers; but if poorly housed and compelled to pick up their living from the slush of the barnyard, they are probably the poorest of the popular breeds. The cocks when grown weigh about six, and the hens, about four pounds.

RHODE ISLAND REDS

The above is one of the promising new breeds that has recently sprung into prominence. It is in size and appearance much on the order of the Buff Rock or the Buff Cochin, except that it is nearest and more trim in its make-up, and in color is of a decidedly rich, handsome, radish brown. "The chicks are almost invariably disappointing, with their variously colored feathers, looking like a miserable lot of little mongrels. They often do not show what they are until after the first molt. As a rule they become richer and redder in color as they grow older. With us they are most excellent layers, good sitters, rapid growers, and I believe with others, that they are one of the coming all-purpose breeds.

"As has been stated, these are the fowl that have done the best for us, but they are by no means the only good breeds that are likely to succeed in this locality. Indeed, I have found this to be true: that a person will succeed best with the breed he likes best; that is, a passionate lover of the Brown Leghorns, who has a disdain for the White, will never succeed with the White; and so on with the various breeds. So we strongly advise that you select, from a list of varieties, the breeds you like best, and give them all the attention that theoretical and practical education will afford, and you cannot but succeed.

HOUSING
"After selecting the desired breed, the kind of house is the next thing in importance, which in this climate need not be expensive, but it should be well built and not be a veritable death trap as so many so-called houses are.

HATCHING CHICKS WITH HENS
 For the average farmer or poultry raiser this is by far the safest and best method. Beware of the person who tells you that artificial incubation and brooding is a "dead easy thing," and that anyone with ordinary intelligence can do it. Such a person is either too ignorant to

know the real difficulties that stand in his way or has become an expert by study and experience.

## SELECTING THE EGGS FOR HATCHING

There are a great many ideas in vogue regarding the size, shape, color etc., of eggs suitable for hatching. Many of these ideas have been proved to be without foundation. The following, however, are safe rules to observe: 1. Never select abnormally large eggs. 2. Never select abnormally small eggs. 3. Never select lop-sided eggs. 4. Never select thin-shelled eggs. 5. Never select an egg with a shell that is ridged or defective in any way. 6. Do not set eggs over two weeks old. 7. Keep eggs for hatching in cool, dry place, and every other day roll them over gently with the hands. 8. Do not handle the eggs with greasy or soiled hands. 9. Handle with great care so that the shells will not be scratched or injured. 10. As far as possible and practical select and set eggs of one breed; that is, do not mix eggs from Leghorns, Rocks, Reds, etc., in the same setting, as they invariably hatch better when kept separate. 11. Always select eggs from active, healthy, and well-mated fowls. Such eggs are usually fertile. Eggs laid by pullets and at the beginning and end of the laying period rarely ever hatch well, and still more rarely produce strong, vigorous birds.

## NUMBER OF EGGS TO SET

his depends almost wholly upon the size of the hen and the condition of the weather. The cooler the weather, the fewer the eggs can be covered with safety. The numbers range from 12 to 15. Broken eggs should be removed from the nest at once and the remaining eggs and nest cleaned. If everything has been looked after properly, in 21 days you may look for a large percentage of good, strong little biddies.

## CARE OF YOUNG CHICKS

"Very early in the spring the chicks must be carefully Page 155 guarded against rain, heavy dews, and kept off the cold, wet ground.

Under the above conditions it is best to keep the hen and her brood in some building. During most of the season an out-door coop is all that is necessary. It is highly important that this coop be made cat and rat proof, as cats, opossums, minks, weasels, etc., will destroy the little chicks in great numbers unless protected.

FEEDING YOUNG CHICKS

From the first period till the chicks are four weeks old, the subject of feeding is quite a problem. Unless it is done with care the death rate will be exceedingly high. This is especially true with incubator chicks.

When the chicks are from 24 to 36 hours old they should have their meal of food. Prior to this a pan of finely powdered charcoal and sand, in the proportion of two-thirds charcoal and one-third sand, is placed before them.

Poultry raisers almost universally agree that, for the first two or three days, hard-boiled eggs is the ideal food for baby chicks. For this they use the fertile eggs from the incubators, boiling them for half an hour. After this they run them through a meat-chopper, grinding them real fine, shells and all. Some mix a little chick grit with it. This is especially recommended where shale sand is not plentiful.

LAYERS AND BREEDERS

There is such a vast difference between fowl kept for laying purposes and those kept to produce eggs for hatching that I deem a few words along this line will be quite acceptable. While no hard and rigid methods can be laid down this fact is apparent: that for laying purposes only, the flock may range from 50 to 100 birds. No male should be allowed with them as they lay better without.

For breeding purposes flocks of 10 to 15 hens and one male bird give the best result as a rule. Each poultry keeper will have to accommodate the size of his flock to his own particular circumstances, being careful not to overdo or underdo too far.

FEEDING FOR EGGS AND FERTILITY

 The Cyphers Incubator Company feeds five evening in the week a mash made as follows: Corn and oat chop . . . . . 40 pounds. Heavy bran . . . . . 30 pounds. Fancy middlings . . . . . 20 pounds. Beef scraps from . . . . . 10 or 15 pounds.     Just enough fluid (water) is used to stick the mash together. Feed a liberal quantity, but not gorge. Scatter plenty of corn, oats and other grain in a litter at night so that they can begin scratching early in the morning. POULTRY DISEASES

Of the almost innumerable number of diseases catalogued by some poultry men, they can be mastered with proper care, and by faithfully following the directions for cleanliness and those given under each disease.

# CHAPTER XVI.
# THE TOMATO AND ITS USE

But few people realize what an important vegetable the tomato is. While it is true that chemical analysis does not place it very high in the nutritive scale, if viewed from this angle alone its real value will be greatly underestimated. For the reasons which follow, every normal person should make the tomato a very prominent part of the weekly diet:

1. It is a vegetable that is easily grown.
2. It yields well and keeps for a long time.
3. It usually brings a fair price, because nearly everyone likes tomatoes.
4. It contains distinct medicinal virtues which are recognized by many authoritative books on household remedies, as "vegetable calomel."
5. It is both a relish and an appetizer as well as a food.
6. Our soils can be made to bring enormous yields of tomatoes, superior in look, taste, and general appearance.
7. They can be prepared in so many delicious ways that one can eat them every day in the week and not get tired of them.
8. The old vines contain splendid dye-stuffs, which could be utilized as a by-product for dying fabrics of various kinds.
9. There are so many sizes, colors, and varieties that, for garnishing's, fancy soups, and especially fine decorative table-effects, they are almost indispensable.

SELECTION OF SOIL

The tomato is not at all choice in the kind of soil in which it grows; in fact, almost any well-drained soil can be made to produce good tomatoes. However, for early ripening, it shows a preference for a light, loamy soil; and, if very early tomatoes are desired, the soil must be only moderately rich, as a highly-fertile soil produces large vines and more fruit, which is likely to delay ripening of the tomatoes.

It is most essential that the ground be spaded or plowed up very deep, harrowed and re-plowed if necessary, until every large cold is mashed, and the ground is fine and mellow.

Do not plant tomatoes on land that has had white potatoes, melons, or tomatoes on it the year previous. Indeed, it is best to let the land rest from these crops three or four years, as all of them are subject to the same blight disease.

FERTILIZERS

It is a mistake to think that the tomato does not like a rich soil. Indeed, to have the best tomatoes, the soil must be rich. The plant is very partial to a soil full of well-rotted vegetable matter; hence, we recommend the following fertilizers, based upon experiments carried out here on the Experiment Station grounds, which gave excellent results:

Two loads of leaves from the forest and muck from the swamp were spread over the bottom of a pen; then one load of barnyard manure. This was continued until the pen was full, and rounded over at the top like a potato hill, so as to present the excess of water from washing out the fertilizing constituents. To this heap old rags, plaster, lime, paper, wood-ashes, finely-beaten-up bones, etc., can be advantageously added.

Make this compost heap in the fall so it will be well rotted by spring.

STARTING THE TOMATO PLANT

In the northern part of West Virginia and in the higher altitudes the tomato seed should be sown from the first to the fifteenth of March, but in the southern part and along the Ohio and Kanawha rivers the seed may be sown as early as February fifteenth.

The best method of starting the plants is by use of a hotbed. It may be constructed as follows: Select a well-drained location where the bed will be sheltered, preferably on the south side of a building or fence. Dig a pit 3 feet wide by 6 feet long and 2 feet deep, so that the long side faces the south. Line the inside of the pit with boards. A stake may be driven in at each corner to serve as a support for the frame, if boards cannot be obtained for lining. Fill the pit with fresh horse manure well packed down by tramping. Construct a frame 3 feet wide by 6 feet long. Have this frame 12 inches high at back or north side and 6 inches high at the front or south side. Place the frame over the pit and bank the outside with strawy manure or soil.

Place in the frame four or five inches of good garden loam which has not grown any disease plants. Cover the bed with glass hotbed sash, unbleached muslin or cheesecloth may be substitutes for the glass.

The fresh horse manure is used to furnish heat for the plants. No seed should be planted until the temperature of the soil falls to 80 degrees F.

If a crop of tomatoes for early market is desired, transplanting is necessary. In this case use two or three rows across the end of the hot-bed for sowing the seed, and use the remainder of the bed for transplanting.

Mark off rods from three to six inches apart and one-fourth inch deep. Drill in the tomato seed, about 12 seeds to the inch. Level the soil and press the surface of the bed firmly and uniformly. Moisten the ground thoroughly.

During summer days ventilate by raising the cover a few inches on the side opposite the wind. Toward evening close the sash in order to get the bed warm before night. As the plants grow older the ventilation may be increased. Water in the mornings on bright days only. Keep the bed moist but not wet. Ventilate after watering in order to dry off the plants.

When the seedlings are about two inches high, or just before the second leaves set, transplant them two inches apart each way to another part of the bed. Another transplanting four inches apart should be made in about three weeks. If there is no remaining space in the hot-bed, a cold frame, constructed similar to the hot-bed except that no pit or manure is necessary, may be used. The seedings may be transplanted to small boxes or flats about 18 inches long, 12 inches wide, and 2½ inches deep and then the boxes placed in the hot-bed or the cold frame.

If the tomatoes are to be canned, principally, it is not necessary to hasten the maturing of all the plants. In that case the hot-bed may be used without any transplanting. Mark off rows four inches apart and one-fourth inch deep. Place one seed every two inches in the row and then transplant every other seeding to another part of the hot-bed or place the seeds at distancs of four inches and do not transplant. Allow these to grow as they stand, until ready for the field.

Before the seedlings are set in the garden plot they should be hardened off by a scant supply of water for several days and by the absence of any covering at night, when there is no danger of frost. Moisten well just before transplanting.

STARTING THE SEED

For a family garden, saw an ordinary cracker-box half in two so it will not be more than six or seven inches deep; nearly fill with good, rich earth, sow the seed; sift earth over them until well covered; water thoroughly, and set in a sunny window. They will soon come up and grow off rapidly. Set out doors on warm days to make them hardy, strong, and stalky.

For a later planting sow out-of-doors, in this latitude about April 15th.

SETTING THE PLANTS

Lay off rows with a middle-burster or two-horse plow; put well-rotted compost in drill at the rate of 25 tons to the acre; bed upon it lightly, and set the tomato directly upon it.

Where a chemical fertilizer is used aim at the following: Cottonseed meal . . . . . 800 pounds Acid phosphate . . . . . 850 pounds Nitrate of soda . . . . . 50 pounds    The nitrate of soda to be applied as a top dressing. Just as the tomatoes begin to set, 250 pounds of muiate of potash is desirable, but at present it is out of the question. For this reason I strongly urge the compost.

SELECTION OF VARIETIES

Every year adds to the long list of varieties of the tomato. With many of these so-called varieties there is a distinction with but little or no difference.

The following varieties have done exceedingly well here on our trial grounds:

EXTRA EARLY VARIETIES:

Spark's Earliana, June Pink, Burpee's Early Pink, John Baer, Prosperity, Bodgian's I. X. L., and Chalk's Early Jewel.

MID-SUMMER VARIETIES: My Maryland, Greater Baltimore, Dwarf Champion, and New Stone.

LATE VARIETIES: Red Rock, Acme, Livingstone's Stone.

CULTIVATING

Tomatoes like the soil about them kept loose and mellow by frequent hoeing, and at one time must they be allowed to become weedy, as weeds greatly injure the plants. A little commercial fertilizer or a quart of compost dug in round the vines once per month will give finger tomatoes and prolong the life of the vines.

CAUTION--Do not use fresh or unrotted manure, as it encourages diseases of various kinds.

# CHAPTER XVII. THE COW PEA

Among the many rich blessings especially given to the South, there are but few, if any, that stand out more prominently than the cow pea, for the following reasons:

1. It is a legume (pod-bearing plant), and brings fertility to the soil. In this it has but few equals, and still fewer superiors.

2. As a food for man and best the peas are almost indispensable, and the vines make a very superior roughage for stock.

3. Year by year this splendid vegetable becomes more popular--the radius over which it is grown has steadily increased until there is scarcely a section of the country where farming is carried on to any considerable degree, that it may not be found in some one or more of its several varieties as forming one of the principal crops.

4. There are few crops grown by the farmer that has such a wide range of uses.

5. It is one of the easiest of farm crops grown, making a fair yield under absolute neglect.

6. It is one sure crop the farmer can depend upon year after year if he plants two or more of the standard varieties.

7. In this locality fresh green peas may be had from the latter part of May until frost.

8. Thus far the demand has been far greater than the supply; hence, prices have always been good.

9. For green-manuring it is universally grown and admired.

10. When the running varieties are planted with corn sorghum, etc., it makes a very superior silage, greatly relished by all kinds of stock.

11. The cow pea rightly handled is both a bank and a mortgage-lifted to the poor man. Page 163

HISTORY

For nearly one hundred years the cow pea has been the chief leguminous (pod bearing) crop throughout the entire group of Southern States. About fifty varieties have been cultivated to a greater or lesser extent in the United States, and every year its value is becoming better known and more highly appreciated, as is evidenced by the increased acreage planted wherever it can be grown.

ORIGIN

Of the large number of varieties cultivated in this country, it is thought that the most of them are of American origin, and they are technically classified as "Vigna Unguiculata." It is also believed that many of the American varieties originated by hybridization or by mutation. The cow pea is closely related to the Catjang family (Vigna Catjang); also to the Asparagus began (Vigna Sesquipedalis). Their cultivation is very ancient especially in Southern Asia and Africa.

There are a great many varieties in those countries, which are being brought over to this country, and from which we may expect some new and valuable crosses. Mr. George W. Oliver has made many hybrids in which the valuable qualities of the two types are combined, and will give us doubtless a more superior pea than either parent. The cow pea is also found growing wild in India. The foreign types are supposed to have been brought to this country from England, in 1734, by Oglethrope and distributed to the Georgia colonies. VARIETIES Of the many varieties upon the market, our Station has found these to be the best for this locality: FOR EARLY PLANTING--Extra Early Black-Eye, New Era Lady, Cuban Blackeye (just a little later than the others).

FOR MID-SUMMER--Iron, Speckled, Groot, Black, Clay, Red Ripper, Brabham, White Crowder.

For late planting nothing was better than the unknown. It made a tremendous growth of vines, and also a good yield of peas.

CLIMATE AND SOIL
In these two particulars Macon County is especially fortunate. While the pea will adjust itself to almost any kind of soil, and will produce larger returns in the way of a crop on thin sandy soils than any other of our common garden or field crops, it delights in a light, well-drained, porous sandy soil. Our own climate is quite ideal--The hot summer sun and the mild winters make the pea almost indigenous. Very often peas lay in the ground all winter and come up in the spring.

SELECTION OF SEED
As a rule, there is practically no attention given to the proper kind of seed to select for planting, and many do not even attempt to keep the different varieties separate. This is a great mistake. It is just as important to select the proper kind of pea for planting as it is to select that of any other farm crop. The following points should be observed:

1. Screen, winnow, float, or hand-pick so as to get only the largest, soundest, and plumpest seed. It is true that many of the small, light, inferior-looking peas will grow and often produce considerable vine, but the yield of peas will be deficient both in quantity and quality.

2. Select peas that are as little eaten by the weevil as possible, and do not be deceived by the old antiquated idea that bug-eaten peas grow just as well as thoroughly sound ones. Two or three small hodes do not seem to materially injure them for planting, but anything above that should not be used if a full crop is expected. The two large fleshy seed leaves contain the stored-up food for the tiny plantlet until it is large enough and strong enough to get its food from the

soil; hence, if these seed leaves have been proportion to the extent of the injury to the seed leaves.

3. Do not plant a conglomerated mixture, but separate the varieties, even if you have to hand-pick them. No two varieties are exactly alike in growth and other characteristics, hence, if sown together, the strongest grower and feeder will more or less overcome the weakest, which means a reduction in the crop in the end, besides the loss of the particular varieties which enter into the admixture.

4. Mixed peas always sell for less than pure varieties, and are never so good for table use, as they do not cook evenly.

The cow pea likes an especially deep and well-prepared seed bed. Prepare exactly the same as for corn or cotton by plowing from 8 to 9 inches deep. Harrow thoroughly, cross-plow, and re-harrow if necessary to put the land in proper condition. The cow pea is a voracious feeder, and the roots travel five and six feet, and even greater distance (under favorable circumstances) in search of food. It must be borne in mind that if the land has been skimmed in the matter of plowing for some years to a depth of three or four inches, do not plow but two inches deeper the first time, unless you have plenty of manure to broadcast and turn under. The next time the land is prepared for a crop, go the other two or three inches as the case may be.

PLANTING

In this there are several methods in common use, all of which, under certain favorable conditions, do well; but experience seems to emphasize the following as points to be observed: Method (a) prepares the ground; puts the seed in with a drill, or sows them by hand, putting from 1½ to 2 bushels per acre, and covers with a harrow. This is all right provided the ground is reasonably rich and well-prepared; the peas will get ahead of the weeds and grass. Do not sow peas in very poor land that has a tendency to bake after the first rain.    Method (b) plants in rows the same as for corn or cotton, and cultivates almost entirely throughout the growing season. This method will produce a good crop of peas, but at too great an expense of labor.

Method (c) plants in rows thus: Lay off two rows by the usual width, say three feet; then another from 12 to 16 inches from it. This will allow the cultivator to run between the rows and keep them clean until the plants get a start. By removing a tooth from a cultivator on the order of the Diverse, both the wide and narrow row may be cultivated at the same time. One or two workings is all that is necessary, as the peas will soon cover the ground and appear as sowed.

This is pre-eminently the method to follow in planting poor land, as it keeps the ground loose, the weeds down, and gives the peas a chance to start growing such as they would not have if sown.

Method (d) plants peas in corn, about the last plowing. They are sown, drilled or chopped in with a hoe as the planter wishes. Often an excellent crop of peas can be made in this way, and at the same time the land is greatly improved.

Sowing with sorghum millet is quite common, and on rich soil, the results are excellent, but exceedingly bad and disappointing on poor soil.

The cow pea belongs to a section of plants known as "legumes," and they characterize themselves from all other plants by bearing pods, in which the seeds are contained. There are two chief reasons why these legumes hold first place with every progressive farmer. First, they have, as no other class of plants have, the power under the proper conditions, to extract nitrogen from the air and impart or give it to the soil. Repeated experiments prove that an acre of well-grown cow peas will, if the total crop is returned, impart from $29 to $30 worth of fertility to the soil. The pea, like all other plants of its class, has the power to extract and use the free nitrogen from the air by certain germs known as bacteria (which belong to the lowest order of plant life). These bacteria collect in large numbers and form nodules (swellings) on the roots. The bacteria collect the nitrogen from the air and deposit it in these nodules, where it is worked over and made ready for the use of the plant. Hence, peas do not require heavy applications of fertilizers containing nitrogen, but they are heavy feeders on potash and phosphoric acid. On exceedingly poor soils it is wise to put a little nitrogen, say 30 or 40 pounds of nitrate of soda per acre, or its equivalent in any other fertilizer containing nitrogen. Where the soil is reasonably rich, as indicated by a heavy growth of vines, no nitrogen is needed.

INOCULATION
Inoculation is the process of supplying the soil with the particular germs (bacteria) that form the nodules. There are two ways in common use that have proved quite satisfactory: First, by getting some soil from a field where the crop was fine and the roots unusually thick with nodules. The soil is loaded into a wagon and scattered out upon the land much the same as for coarse fertilizers. The peas are then planted in the usual manner. This method is universally satisfactory. Second, by the use of commercially prepared preparation known as pure cultures. A full set of directions accompany each bottle or package of material, so that all that is necessary is to carry them out.

The second reason for their great popularity is that the seeds are very rich in nitrogenous (muscle-building) material; so therefore, there is no foodstuff to take its place--none that will answer just as well from every point of view for feeding all kinds of animals.

CULTIVATION
When sown broadcast they require no cultivation. When in drills, as heretofore referred to, they are greatly improved by two or three shallow workings, sufficient to keep the weeds down and the soil mellow. They will soon cover the ground.

HARVESTING
As a hay crop, the cow pea should be to the South what the red clover is to the North.        The steams are quite succulent, and care

must be taken or the leaves will drop off before the stems are sufficiently dry to store away.

When to Cut.--The best time to cut is when the first pods begin to turn yellow. There are a great variety of ways to save the hay, many of which are good, but I like this one the best. Never cut a large quantity down when the weather is threatening rain, as the curing process cannot be rushed as in other hays.

Begin cutting as early in the morning as the dew is off. (Never cut wet vines for hay as they are almost sure to spoil). As soon as the top vines are thoroughly wilted, run over them with a hay-tedder or something that will turn them. A pitch fork is excellent, but slower and more laborious. If the weather is favorable the hay may be put into small cocks the next afternoon, leaving it thus three or four days before hauling it to the barn. A good plan is to take some of the largest stems between the thumbs and fingers, giving them a severe twist; if any juice appears, it is too wet to stack or bale.

Those who have had such experience with saving pea-vine hay know that there are two danger points--under-drying, which causes moulding and rotting when stored; over-drying, which causes all the leaves to drop off in handling so that there is nothing but a pile of stems when the storage place is reached. In either case the feeding value is greatly impaired or wholly destroyed.

Pea-vine hay goes through a sweating process, and therefore should be put into small stacks, tipping the stacks with hay, straw, or some such material sufficiently deep to turn the water. Allow it to remain in these two or three weeks.

For stock this would make a feed unsurpassed in milk, flesh, and fat-forming properties, and I am sure it would be at a cost below the average mixed feed. In fact, if the vines have many peas on them and the whole is ground up together, it is almost a complete balance ration within itself.

AS FOOD FOR MAN
As food for man, it may be prepared in a sufficient number of ways to suit the most fastidious palate. Page 169

# CHAPTER XVIII.
# THREE DELICIOUS MEALS EVERY DAY

The true housekeeper in planning meals, sometimes experiences difficulty in finding foods which contain the maximum amount of nutriments for the minimum expenditure of money. A knowledge of food values helps in planning meals that are economical. Therefore, every housekeeper will find this chapter very helpful and useful.

Even cheap foods properly prepared and daintily served are more palatable. Plain, wholesome and nutritious foods can be prepared easily each day in the week, from the following:

MONDAY (breakfast) Granulated toast, served with cream, sugar and peaches. Strawberries, Figs, Blackberries, Stewed pears, or fruit of some kind, either fresh or dried. (This makes a delicious and inexpensive breakfast dish). Bacon and eggs, Biscuit, Coffee (made from velvet beans, cow peas or soy beans, if you desire). Butter, milk.

MONDAY (dinner) Vegetable soup (from chicken bones). Cabbage or collards, boiled with bacon, sweet potatoes, baked. Egg corn bread. Sweet or sour milk; butter; blackberry pie.

MONDAY (supper) Light bread and butter; fruit, jelly, or jam of some kind. Bacon puffs, served with syrup; tea, milk.

TUESDAY (breakfast) Stewed or fresh fruit, served with cream; egg omelet, served with ham; corn muffins; butter; syrup; milk; coffee and sliced tomatoes.

TUESDAY (dinner) Pea soup, with toast bread, (sippet). Roast pork, with sweet or white potatoes; cream onions; corn bread; fresh buttermilk; butter; bread pudding, served with cream.

TUESDAY (supper) Cold sliced ham (or cold meat of any kind). Green-corn croquettes or fritters (canned corn or dried corn can be used). Sliced tomatoes and onions. White bread and corn pone; milk; tea; butter and syrup.

WEDNESDAY (breakfast)
Granulated toast, with cream and fruit; home-made sausages or meat balls; batter cakes, with syrup; sliced tomatoes; milk; butter and coffee. WEDNESDAY (dinner)

Creamed peas; turnips or rutabugas, boiled with bacon; salad, made of shredded cabbage; lettuce, onion; tomatoes; cucumbers; green peppers (sweet) and parsely; garnish with hardboiled egg. Corn batter bread. Sweet and sour milk; butter; sliced sweet potato pie.

WEDNESDAY (supper)
Ripe tomatoes sliced, and fried. Cream hash on toast. Page 171 White bread; butter and syrup. Sweet milk; tea; peaches, with cream. Plain molasses; cookies or cake.

THURSDAY (breakfast)
Baked apples or pears, served with cream and toast. Liver, smothered in onions, with cream gravy. Hot biscuit; butter; milk; coffee; fresh mush; grits, or rice.

THURSDAY (dinner)
Cream of tomato soup. Roast beef, with sweet or white potatoes. Succotash of lima beans and corn. Fatty corn; fresh buttermilk; peach; apple, or berry pie, served with cream.

THURSDAY (supper)
Sweet potatoes, sliced and fried with minced meat. White bread; lye hominy; sliced tomatoes. Fruit, with cream, ginger bread; milk and tea.

FRIDAY (breakfast)

Granulated toast, with fruit and cream. Ham and egg; corn or wheat muffins; milk; butter and coffee.

FRIDAY (dinner)
A rich vegetable soup; peas boiled with bacon; egg bread; sliced cucumbers; onions, and tomatoes. Sweet or sour milk. Blackberry cobler, served with cream; butter.

FRIDAY (supper)
Bacon puffs, with syrup; tomatoes (bread). White bread and toast; milk; butter; cottage cheese (smear case, homemade). Cookies. Fruit or berries, with cream, and tea.

SATURDAY (breakfast)
Corn meal mush, served with cream and fruit; home-made sausage; hot cakes, with syrup. Toast; milk; butter and coffee.

SATURDAY (dinner)
Cream of tomato; roast pork, with peas; sweet potatoes, baked. Beet pickles. Plain corn bread.

SATURDAY (supper)
Fried egg plant or tomatoes; baked peas; beet salad; syrup; butter; milk and tea.

SUNDAY (breakfast)
Baked apples or pears, served with cream. Breaded pork-chops, smothered in onions. Hot rolls; syrup; butter; milk and coffee.

SUNDAY (dinner)
Chicken pot pie; egg corn bread; boiled cabbage; mixed pickles; string beans. Fresh buttermilk; iced cream; cake; salted peanuts; pecans, walnuts or hickory nuts.

SUNDAY (supper)
Peel tomatoes, stuff with minced meat, served with salad dressing. Nut sandwiches. Fruit, served with cream. Milk and tea.

Granulated toast is simply toast made in the ordinary way, and when nicely browned it may be crushed with a rolling pin, run through a meat chopper, or ground in an ordinary coffee mill. Save every scrap of bread regardless of how small, as it may be used in a variety of ways for stuffing meats. Page

# CHAPTER XIX. FORTY-THREE WAYS TO SAVE THE WILD PLUM CROP

Nature endows or blesses each State or section with an indigenous flora and fauna best suited to that particular soil and climatic conditions.

Applying the above to Alabama, Macon and adjoining counties have been unusually blessed in the quantity and variety of its wild plums.

They vary in size from a half to one inch in diameter, and in flavor from sugary sweetness to sour and bitter. In color, from lemon yellow to crimson, scarlet and black, making possibilities for many pleasing combinations for the eye and palate.

I feel safe in saying that in Macon County alone there are many hundred bushels of plums that go to waste every year that there is a full crop, which is almost one year with another.

In a commercial way there is a great opportunity for jam and jelly factories.

No fruit improves with cultivation more satisfactory than the wild plum; both the size and flavor is improved, and under cultivation some of the yellow and red types compare favorably in size with the wild goose and other cultivated varieties of that class.

In comparison with some of the standard fruits of the world as to food and dietetic value, one is at a loss to know why so valuable a fruit has been and is being so sadly neglected and allowed practically to go to waste.

Name of Fruit Protein Water Muscle Builders Carbohydrates Fat Formers Calories Heat units in one pound Ash Apples 84.6 .4 14.2 .3 290 Blackberries 86.3 1.3 10.0 .5 270 Cherries 80.9 1.0 16.7 .6 365 Pears 84.4 .6 14.2 .4 295 Plums 78.4 1.0 20.1 .5 395

A glance at the above table shows that the plum in some respects is higher in food value than some of the most highly prized fruits in the list.

No fruit makes more delicious jams, jellies, preserves, marmalades, etc., and it is the purpose of this chapter to set forth in a practical way a number of recipes by which every housewife may be successful in the saving of this splendid article of food. NO. 1—

CANNED PLUMS
These may be used for puddings, pies, sauces, tarts, desserts, etc.

Select firm but well ripened fruit, prick the skin in several places to prevent bursting when cooked. Use pound for pound of sugar and fruit where an especially rich sauce is wanted, or eight quarts of plums and two quarts of sugar can be used. Add just water enough to melt the sugar; add a few of the plums at a time, cook until tender, and carefully remove the fruit and place in jars. Fill up with syrup and seal. Set in a dark place and away from draughts of air to prevent the jars from cracking.

NO. 2--PLUM JAM
Select only nice, well ripened fruit; take pound for pound of fruit and sugar; cover the fruit with boiling water; when nearly cold drain and add the sugar; cook slowly, stirring and skimming until it is thick enough for the juice to jelly when Page 175 cold. Pack away in stone jars or glass vessels, store in a dark, cold place, examine from time to time and re-boil if inclined to sour.

NO. 3--PLUM MARMALADE    Prepare the plums the same as for jam; to every pound of plums add one-half of either apples or peaches, cook until thoroughly tender and mash, remove the seed if you wish, by passing through a colander or course sieve. Add one and one-half pounds of sugar to every two pounds of the fruit mixture; boil slowly and skim until it is thick like the jam; season to taste with ground cloves, cinnamon, allspice and just a suggestion of mace and nutmeg. Pack away the same as recommended for jam.

No. 4--MARMALADE NO. 2 (Delicious)
Take fruit as follows: two pounds of plums, one-half pound of apples that have been peeled and cored; one-half pound of mulberries; one-fourth pound of the wild black cherries; one pound of peaches after peeling and "seeding"; one-half pound of blackberries. Wash, drain and add just water enough to keep from burning while cooking, boil until tender; remove the seed and add four and one-half pounds of sugar; boil slowly and skim thoroughly until thick, spice to taste, the same as number one, and pack away the same. This marmalade is excellent with turkey, chicken and all kinds of fresh meat.

NO. 5--PLUM PRESERVES
I have had this method to give most excellent results. Select good, medium, but not over-ripe plums. After the plums have been peeled, which can be easily and quickly done by placing the fruit in boiling water for two or three minutes, and then into cold water, take a stone, porcelain or glass jar and place a layer of sugar and a layer of plums until as full as desired. Let stand overnight, pour off the juice and let come to a boil, skim well, drop the fruit into this hot syrup; Page 176 let it boil slowly until the fruit is clear. Now add to each quart of plums, fifteen grains of whole spice, ten cloves, three sticks of cinnamon an inch long and four shreds of mace. Seal and treat the same as for other fruit.

NO. 6--PLUM, PEACH AND APPLE PRESERVES
Take one pound of plums, one pound of apples and one pound of peaches. All should be peeled and the apples and peaches cut into discs about the size of the plums. Sugar the fruit the same as for plum preserves but in separate jars. After standing over night, drain the syrup from each one into a preserving kettle and boil gently and skim thoroughly for two minutes, put the peaches in first, boil until tender, remove and add the apples, boiling them until tender, remove and add the plums, boiling them until clear. The apples and peaches should be kept hot; the plums should now be added and the whole

mixed together but not mashed. Add spice exactly the same in kind and quality as recommended for preserves.

### NO. 7--PLUM CONSERVE
Take three pounds of peeled plums, one pound of very ripe peaches that have been peeled and sliced. Select three large oranges, remove the seed and mince the pulp. Grate the rinds and use the pulp and juice. Put all together and stir in three and one-half pounds of granulated sugar and one-half pound of strained honey; boil slowly until thick and seal hot.

### NO. 8--PLUM JELLY
Take as many medium ripe plums as you wish, cover them with boiling water. Pour off immediately, draining them thoroughly. Put them into a preserving kettle with just boiling water enough to cover them, boil until the plums begin to burst and considerable juice extracted. Pour off liquid and strain, for each pound of juice add one pound of white sugar. Return to the kettle and boil it slowly for twenty or thirty minutes, as it may require. Pour into jelly glasses Page 177 and set aside to cool. When solid cover closely and store in a cold, dry place.

### NO. 9--PICKLED PLUMS NO. 1
Take either the yellow or red varieties when just ripe but not mushy, wash and dry with a soft cloth, prick them a few times; place in a stone jar, add four and one-half pounds of sugar to one gallon of vinegar (of medium strength). Put into preserving kettle, boil and skim several times. Continue heating the vinegar and pouring over them every other day for three days.

### NO. 10--PICKLED PLUMS NO. 2
Take seven pounds of plums and five pounds of brown sugar, one-fourth pound of stick cinnamon; two ounces of cloves and two ounces of allspice; scald just vinegar enough to cover them and pour over the spiced plums four mornings in succession. Pack in glass or stone vessels. Caution--Do not put in vessels with metal tops.

NO. 11--PLUM JUICE
Select only well ripened plums for the finest flavored vinegar. Prepare kettle and crush with a wooden pestle. Heat slowly and boil gently for about twenty-five minutes. Crush again; put two thicknesses of cheesecloth into the colander, pour in and let drain; when sufficiently cold, press out all the juice possible by twisting the cloth. Clean the preserving kettle and return the juice to the fire. When it boils draw back and skim, repeat this three or four times. To every pint of juice add one-half pint of sugar; boil five or six minutes, skimming carefully. Fill hot sterilized jars or bottles. Set the vessel in boiling water and allow it to simmer for twenty-five minutes; re-fill with boiling juice; remove from fire and seal. Place on boards and set in a dark place out of a draft. This makes a delicious beverage when properly diluted and used the same as grape juice.

NO. 12--A CHEAP AND DELICIOUS PLUM PUDDING Take: 2 quarts corn meal, 1 quart stoned plums cut into pieces, 1 pound chopped suet, 1 tablespoon butter, 8 eggs beaten up into sufficient milk to make the whole into a stiff batter. Put into a bag and boil three hours; serve with any kind of sauce you like. This pudding can be saved in a cool place, and warmed over, day after day, and is as nice as when fresh.

NO. 13--PLUM SYRUP
Make exactly the same as recommended for plum juice except three-fourths as much sugar as juice must be added. This is excellent for water ices, ice cream, etc. Two or three spoonfuls added to a glass of ice water is very refreshing in hot weather.

NO. 14--PLUM VINEGAR
Select only well ripened plums for the finest flavored vinegar. Prepare the same as for jelly except the pulp may be washed twice with warm water so as to extract just as much of the juice a spossible. Pour into stone or glass vessels and set into warm place for two days. Skim and decant the clear liquid, and to every three pints of juice add one pint of brown sugar. Pour into jugs; tie a cloth over

the top and set in a dark place to work. When sufficiently strong it may be corked and put away for use. A little "mother" from strong vinegar is often added with excellent results.

NO. 15—DRIED PLUMS NO. 1
Select medium ripe plums, cover with boiling water, cover the vessel and let stand twenty minutes; drain and spread in the sum to dry. Stir occasionally, when dry examine them Page 179 frequently and at the first appearance of worms put in the oven and heat for a few minutes. In cooking, soak in cold water for a few hours the same as for other dried fruit.

NO. 16--DRIED PLUMS NO. 2

After peeling the plums, allow half pound of sugar to one pound of fruit. Put fruit and sugar in layers in a preserving kettle. Heat slowly until the sugar is dissolved, then boil until clear. Spread the fruit on platters in the sun and turn often until quite dry. Pack in layers with sugar in stone or glass jars. Plums dried in this way are extra fine.

NO. 17--PLUMS AS OLIVES
Take plums when just beginning to ripen, but still green, make a brine out of sea salt, if possible--common rock salt will do--strong enough to hold up an egg. Pour the brine over the fruit hot. Cover and let stand for twenty-four hours. Pour off and make a new brine, in which place the fruit, boil one minute and seal in the hot brine. NO.

18--PLUM SOUP NO. 1
Take one-half teacup of rice, soak overnight, add two quarts of cold water, boil until thoroughly done and pasty, peel and stew a pint of well ripe plums, pass through a colander to remove the seeds; sweeten to taste, add to the rice paste, add a little cinnamon, one clove and a dash of nutmeg.

NO. 19--PLUM SOUP NO. 2

Take one pint of ripe plums and one quart of blackberries, stew each separately, until thoroughly done, rub plums through colander and rub the blackberries through a sieve just fine enough to remove the seed; boil two tablespoons of tapioca thoroughly done in two quarts of water, mix, return to the fire, and simmer twenty-five minutes. Add a little cinnamon, sweeten with sugar to taste, or add a little salt as preferred. Serve cold.

NO. 20--PLUM SOUP NO. 3
Make exactly as for number two, except a pint of very ripe peaches must be added that have been peeled and reduced to a pulp without cooking. Sweeten to taste and serve, preferably with cream and sugar. NO.

21--PLUM LOZENGES NO. 1
Take one-third pint of sugar to each pint of thick plum juice after straining; allow to simmer thirty-five to forty minutes, when at boiling point add two heaping tablespoons of gelatine that has been previously dissolved in a very little cold water, stir well, remove from the fire and continue to stir until it begins to cool and thicken. Pour into well-buttered plates or earthen dishes, let dry slowly, sprinkle with sugar during the process, when sufficiently dry cut into any shape desired.

NO. 22--PLUM LOZENGES NO. 2 (Very fine)
Take one pint of sugar, one pint each of thick plum, peach and blackberry juice; simmer and skim for thirty minutes, when at boiling point add three heaping tablespoons of gelatine that has been previously soaked in a little cold water. Treat the same as for No. 1. Until nearly ready to cut, sprinkle and immerse bits of candied plums and peaches; cut piece to include one or both of these choice tid-bits.

NO. 23--WILD PLUM CATSUP
To each five pounds of plums take two and one-half pounds of sugar, cooking, crushing, and putting through the sieve. To each quart of juice add a generous half-pint of vinegar and spice to taste. Cook twenty minutes and bottle.

NO. 24--PLUM PASTE

Select very ripe plums, put into a granite or porcelain lined stew kettle, and add two tablespoons of water, cover tightly Page 181 and steam very slowly until enough water forms to allow them to cook slowly without burning. Boil until they can be rubbed to a pulp, pass through a sieve to remove the seed, return the pulp to the fire and cook slowly until very thick, add one-half of its weight of brown sugar; let dissolve and boil for a few minutes, pour the mass into earthen plates or dishes, in quarter or inch thicknesses, and dry slowly in a war moven. Remove when sufficiently dry and pack away, to be used in puddings, candies, cakes, etc.

NO. 25--PLUM ROLL

Use very ripe plums the same as for the paste. Mash and remove the pits, pour into platters about one-fourth inch thick, add sugar slowly as long as it will absorb any, dry in a moderate oven, remove the thin sheets from the platters, dust with powdered sugar and roll, put in bags or jars for use. It is ready for use after soaking for a few hours in cold water, usually without cooking and without sugar.

NO. 26--PLUM ROLY-POLY

This can be made with either plum paste, or the plum prepared as for Betty, as follows: make a sweet biscuit dough, roll out thin and spread with a large layer of plums, sprinkle with sugar, butter and spice and roll the dough over as for jelly roll. Steam two hours or bake in a moderate oven.

NO. 27--PLUM DUMPLINGS BAKED

Remove the seed from the desired number of thoroughly ripe plums, roll out biscuit dough quite thin, cut in squares enough to cover four or six plums, sprinkle with a tablespoon of sugar, bring up the corners of the dough and fasten by pinching and twisting together. Place in baking pan close together and when pan is full pour over them a syrup made with one pint of water and three-fourths pound of sugar, letting it come half way to the top of the dumplings. Cinnamon, allspice and a dash of nutmeg may be sprinkled over the top of each. Bake fifty minutes in rather a brisk oven. Serve with cream or hard sauce.

## NO. 28--PLUM CROQUETTES NO. 1
Prepare the plums the same as for the paste, further thicken with fine bread crumbs or cracker dust, minced walnuts, hickory nuts or nuts of any kind add greatly to its flavor; stir in additional sugar if desired, and a dash of spice. Roll in egg, then in crumbs, fry a deep brown in boiling fat.

## NO. 29--PLUM BETTY
Select two or three cups of very ripe plums; remove the seed and mince very fine. Butter a dish, put in a layer of plums, sprinkle with cinnamon, sugar and butter, cover with bread crumbs, alternate the layers of fruit and crumbs as long as desired, stopping with layer of crumbs. Do not add water, but cover tight and steam one hour in a moderate oven, after which remove the cover and brown quickly. Serve with cream sauce.

## NO. 30--PLUM DUMPLINGS BOILED
Prepare the plums the same as for baked dumplings, tie each one in a separate cloth, plung into boiling water and boil vigorously for one-half hours. Serve with cream or hard sauce.

## NO. 31--PLUM DUMPLINGS IN CUPS
Line baking cups with thin pastry; fill with seeded plums and sugar; place on each a cover of the pastry and put them in a large baking pan, pouring boiling water around the cups half way up; bake until done in a hot oven.

## NO. 32--DELICIOUS PLUM TART
Seed and place in a crock without any water the desired amount of plums; put in a slow oven and cook until tender, Page 183 mix half and half with peaches that have been peeled, seeded and treated in the same way. Place in baking dish, sugar to taste, cover with a sheet of well pricked pastry and bake quickly, serve cold with cream, or rich milk.

NO. 33--PLUM SANDWICHES
Spread thin slices of bread with plum jam or plum paste, sprinkle liberally with chopped hickory nuts, walnuts, chestnuts, etc. If desired very rich, spread the bread with butter before putting on the fruit and chopped nuts.

NO. 34--PLUM SHORT-CAKE WITH NUTS (Very Rich)     Make a rich pie crust, roll out thin and bake; cut any shape desired and proceed as follows: Select very ripe plums, peel, seed and chop very fine; sweeten to taste; spread a thin layer over each piece of pastry, in the same manner as for layer cake; sprinkle each layer liberally with minced nuts. Build up as high as you desire, ice the top and decorate artistically with nut kernals. Serve with cream or very rich milk.

NO. 35--PLUM CROQUETTES NO. 2
Take the desired amount of plum paste or plum and peach marmalade; put into a double boiler and let come to the boiling point; have ready about one-third of a cup of corn starch that has been moistened with just a little cold water; stir in and cook fifteen minutes; just before removing add one beaten egg, whipping as it cooks; place all in a flat, wet mould or deep dish and set aside to cool. When needed drop a teaspoon of the mixture into fine dry bread, or cracker crumbs, place in basket and fry to a light brown in boiling fat; spices, nuts and lemon juice may be added if desired.

NO. 36--DELICIOUS PLUM SHERBET
Scald a quart of rich milk, dissolve in a cup of sugar. Let simmer eight minutes, then cool, adding to it (when cold) a pint of plum pulp when sweetened and flavored. When half frozen add whites of two eggs whipped, and complete the freezing. NO. 37--PLUM
ICE     Seed and rub to a pulp the desired amount of well ripened plums; for every pint of plums add three-fourths pint of sugar; let stand two hours. Strain, and to each half gallon of syrup allow one and one-half pint of water. Freeze. The pulp will make nice pies,

tarts, sauce or croquettes by the addition of a little sugar and flavoring to taste.

## NO. 38--PLUM PUDDING
Over a quart of seeded plums sprinkle one and three-fourths pound of sugar; let stand an hour; drain off the juice; add to it a pint of rich sweet milk, four well beaten eggs, a little more sugar if not sweet enough, a tablespoon of butter, melted and rubbed smooth with half a cup of flour, and a little of the milk; add a pinch of salt, pour over the plums and bake till brown; serve with cream or the fruit syrup that was drained off.

## NO. 39--PLUM PUNCH
Seed and mash a pound of very ripe plums, place in bowl with the juice of three lemons and two oranges, and three slices of pineapples; cover with one and one-half pint of sugar. Let stand one hour and strain. Heat this and add a quart each of carbonated water and calaret, a sliced banana and one-fourth pound of candied plums.

## NO. 40--PLUM RICE PUDDING
Allow two tablespoons of rice to one quart of milk slated. Boil together slowly for half a nhour. Then place in the baking dish with one cup of seeded and sweetened plums. Bake an hour, stirring frequently. The last time stir in a half cup of mixed nuts, cover with well beaten egg and brown lightly, serve with cream. Page 185

## NO. 41--OLD-FASHIONED PLUM PIE
Take very ripe plums, seed and put them in a deep pie-plate lined with a rich puff paste, sprinkle a thick layer of sugar on each layer of plums, add spice if desired, put in a tablespoon of water, and sprinkle a little flour over the top. Cover with thick crust and bake from fifty to sixty minutes.

## NO. 42--DRIED PLUM PIE
Soak the desired amount of dried plums in cold water several hours. Stew hours. Stew until tender, thoroughly mash by rubbing through a colander, beat two eggs, saving the white of one, and three-fourths

cup of sugar and one-half cup of butter to every pie, spice to taste, stir in the eggs, line a deep pie-pan with puff paste, fill and bake until done, frost the white of the egg and spread on top, return to a quick oven and brown slightly. NO.

43--FRIED PLUM PIE
Take plain discuit dough, roll out very thin. Put two tablespoons of plum paste or stewed plums that have been spiced and well sweetened. Fold the crust over and cut into small half-moons, wet and crimp the edges. Distribute the fruit by pressing the pie gently after crimping. Fry to a rich brown in boiling hot fat."

# CHAPTER XX. ALFALFA

For many years we have been testing in one way or another almost every variety of legume that seemed in the least promising, with the view of finding one or more that would succeed in this section and give us a permanent pasture without having to prepare and re-seed the ground each year.

LOCATION AND SOIL
In character the soil is a light-gray, sandy, upland, free from lime, underlaid with red and yellow mottled clay, which crops out here and there on the surface. The sand content ranges from 75 to 85 per cent, and is just the kind of soil upon which time-honored custom says alfalfa will not grow.

THE BEGINNING
Early in the summer of 1911 the land was broadcasted with 8 tons of barnyard manure to the acre; plowed to a depth of 9 inches, and sowed in cow peas, which made a heavy growth of vines and an excellent crop of peas. The vines being too heavy were grazed off by the cows, re-manured with 5 tons of barnyard manure to the acre, 5 tons of caustic lime (air slacked), and 5 tons of crushed lime rock per acre. These were plowed in and harrowed thoroughly.

NOTE--Later experiments proved that 2 tons of caustic lime or 3 tons of agricultural lime per acre give just as good results on these soils.

INOCULATING THE SEED
Before beans, peas, clovers, vetches, peanuts, alfalfa, etc., will grow and thrive, the little germs (bacteria) must be present in the soil so they can attach themselves to the roots, Page 187 and form the characteristic swellings called nodules, found in greater or less abundance on all healthy roots of the great pod-bearing family. The act of supplying the young plants with these is called inoculation, and may be done in the following ways:

1. By using a commercial germ, of which there are many now on the market. All that is necessary is to follow the printed rules which always accompany each package.

2. By securing soil from a good alfalfa or sweet-clover field. Scatter evenly over the field from 500 to 600 pounds per acre of this soil. Select a cool, cloudy day to do this work. Sow the seed at once, and harrow or brush it lightly.

3. Where it is difficult to get large quantities of soil secure about a bushel of earth carefully selected from among the roots of thriftiest alfalfa or sweet-clover patches; pass through a coarse sieve to remove the large lumps, trash, etc.; dampen the seed a little; mix the soil with them, and stir constantly until every seed has a little film of earth around it. This can be easily and quickly done by spreading the seed out on a smooth floor. This method has given us excellent results. The seed should be sown at once or spread out in the shade to dry.

SOWING
Select any good, Southern-grown seed if possible, and sow at the rate of 25 pounds per acre, which is very heavy seeding, but it is of distinct value in smothering out the weeds, which are the greatest enemies to alfalfa growers.

CAUTION--Do not inoculate and sow in hot, dry, sunshiny weather, as the germs (bacteria) are very sensitive to excessive heat and bright sunlight, and many would be killed, rendering the inoculation more or less ineffective.

MANAGEMENT
From the very first a war on weeds must be made. If they are very thick and alfalfa small and weak, they must be pulled out by hand. All weak and sickly spots must be remanured, and fresh seed sown. A hand-rake as a rule is sufficient with which to put in the seed on these small patches.

RESULTS   As previously stated, the ground for two acres of alfalfa was prepared as above described; the seed was of the Provence variety, inoculated with Farmo-germ, and sown Nov. 4, 1911.

**NOTE**--Owing to the extreme drought in the fall, this seeding was at least three weeks later than it should have been, as it did not give time enough for the young plants to get sufficiently strong to stand the winter as they should, and much of it froze out.

January 15th it was re-seeded with 15 pounds of seed to the acre. A light scratch harrow was made by driving large spike nails through a plank, making the same a V-shaped harrow. This was run over the ground, and was sufficient to rake the seed in and do little or no injury to the growing plants.

IMPORTANT THINGS TO REMEMBER

1. Be sure the ground is well prepared before sowing.

2. Be sure to get good, clean seed, free from weeds of all kinds. To insure this, purchase only from reliable seed houses.

3. Sow thick so as to smother out the weeds. Hand-pick the largest ones. When the alfalfa gets high enough to bear cutting, let the weeds grow until nearly ready to bloom; then cut them off close to the ground with a mower.

4. Remember that hundreds of acres of alfalfa are killed outright of greatly weakened until the grower concludes it would not grow, and plowed it up, simply because he did not understand when to cut and when to graze.

One of the most valuable characteristics of alfalfa is the strong, heavy crowns, from which a number of new stalks spring. Until alfalfa is three or four years old it should not be cut into these crowns form for the new growth. If one looks carefully he can see them as little buds clustered around the root just above the ground. The leaves on the stalks will also begin to turn yellow and fall off; then it should be cut.

An alfalfa weeder is an excellent thing to run over it, which will dig out the small weeds and loosen up the earth around the plants, and give them new life. An old spring-tooth harrow, with the teeth drawn down almost to a point, makes an excellent substitute for a real weeder.

GRAZING

This should not be done under three or four years, because the crowns are not well developed until that time; and many are the patches killed by being impatient for results and grazing too early. Do not make this mistake and blame something else for your failure.

5. Remember that when you get a good field of alfalfa it is permanent for many years, yielding handsome crops three or five times a year (depending upon the season) or, if wisely done, continuous grazing for all kinds of stock.

6. That there is practically no farm crop richer in real nutrients than alfalfa, and that all kinds of classes of domestic animals will eat it greedily and thrive on it with little or no grain. It is also becoming quite popular as a food for man, and many are the delicacies that frequently find their way upon our tables and just as soon as we learn to appreciate its real value and the methods of preparation become more universal, it will constitute an important part of every well-compounded dietary.

7. Of the great list of agricultural plants that bring fertility to the soil, alfalfa is king of them all.

8. That, if every farmer had a few acres of alfalfa and cattle, sheep, hogs, goats, chickens, horses, mules, etc., to consume it, the manure

from these animals, carefully saved and returned to the soil, within a few years would justify the whole South in boasting of being the richest and most productive section of the United States, if not of the world.

9. Let us hope that every farmer will plan now to put in at least a small acreage of this wonderful plant in the fall.

# CHAPTER XXI. THE PICKLING AND CURING OF MEAT IN HOT WEATHER

Many and varied are the methods of curing and otherwise preserving meat in the fall and winter months when the weather is cold enough to insure success.

All the methods examined were successful and some of superior merit, but the notion of killing and preserving meat in hot weather had scarcely been given a thought; "impossible" seemed to have been written across the face of any such proposition. However, two great problems demanding a solution seemed to be ever before us.

The entire South has been slow in the matter of pork production for the following reasons: First, the foodstuff for fattening hogs is especially plentiful in summer; the hogs grow off and fatten rapidly; they soon reach the killing point, and become a loss in dollars and cents, besides having other disadvantages whenever an attempt is made to carry them over till cold weather. Second, cholera, which rarely fails to make its more or less destructive appearance in the fall, seems to be especially partial to fat hogs.

I think possibly that these two things have done more to keep the South from being a great pork-raising center than all the others combined. With this situation before us, a pickling solution seemed the most feasible; so, therefore, we set about to find one.

A large number were found for the corning or pickling of beef, but these for pork were rather meager; but by taking those available in this and other countries, particularly those found in the United Kingdom of Great Britain, Ireland, Denmark, Holland, Scotland, England and Canada, I was able to work out the following which has worked admirably with us.

## CORN CLUBS

Nothing in recent years has stirred the South from center to circumference, as it were, as has the demonstration movement and the boys' corn clubs. Boys 16 years old have been able to raise from 5, 19, 15, and 20 to 225 bushels per acre. This means more and better stock of all kinds, all of which are indications of greater prosperity.

The suggestions in this chapter, if carefully carried out, should prove a fitting compliment to the Boys' Corn Club movement by the organization of Pig Clubs, and instead of buying most of our pork outside of our borders, sending millions of dollars from home, we shall be able to save these millions by supplying other sections of the country with pickled meat and bacon of superior quality.

## CAUTION
Do not use dirty vessels of any kind--molasses, cottolene, and lard barrels are the best. They should be free from objectionable odors such as vinegar, kerosine, fish, etc., which might spoil the meat.

If meat has ever spoiled in a barrel or any other container, it must be thoroughly washed out and sterilized in some way until every trace of disagreeable odor disappears.

Do not put in meat that has begun to spoil, with the hope of saving it, as it will taint, to a greater or lesser degree, every piece of meat in the container.

## PREPARATION
Kill and dress the meat in the usual manner, being extremely clean and tidy with every operation. Chill for 24 hours in a good refrigerator (if the water is too hot to remove the animal heat without doing so) when left whole, and 12 hours when cut up ready for pickling.

**PROCESS**
After the vessels have been thoroughly cleaned, cover the Page 192 bottom with salt. Rub each piece of meat vigorously with a handful of dry salt, packing the pieces in vessel as tightly as possible. Sprinkle each layer liberally with salt. Fill with meat to the top. Where the pieces are very large it is wise to cut the sides into two or three pieces and cut the hams and shoulders to the bones in several places with a sharp knife.

**PICKLING SOLUTIONS**
Of the several solutions given, the first one following has given us the greatest satisfaction, although you will note that there is very little essential difference in them.

**METHOD NO. 1**
For every 100 lbs. of pork use 8 lbs. of salt, 4 lbs. of brown sugar or 6 lbs. of molasses, 2 ounces of baking soda, 4 ounces of saltpeter in hot weather and 2 or none in cold weather.

Dissolve the above thoroughly in a sufficient amount of tepid water to cover the meat to the depth of four or five inches. Weigh down with a heavy stone. Do not let iron of any kind touch the brine, such as iron weights or nails in the board covers, as all such will impart a disagreeable flavor to the meat. The same is true with an unclean vessel of any kind.

The strength of the brine may be tested by dropping a fresh egg into it.

If the egg floats upon the top, with two-thirds of its body out the brine, it is strong enough; otherwise, more salt must be added.

**METHOD NO. 2  (For Sugar-cured Hams and Bacon)**
This is a universal recipe, and has given satisfaction wherever used. Allow the hog to cool thoroughly before cutting. Trim hams and shoulders, and split the sides in two, lengthwise. Cover the bottom of the barrel with fine salt, and rub each piece of meat thoroughly with

the salt. Pack tightly in a barrel, with hams on the bottom, shoulders next, and sides on top. If the weather is sufficiently cool, allow the meat to stand for three days before putting on the pickling solution; in hot weather put it on at once. For each 100 lbs. of meat weigh out 8 lbs. of salt, 2 lbs. of brown sugar, and 2 ounces of saltpeter; 1 pint of molasses, 1 ounce of cayenne pepper, 1 ounce of black pepper berries (unground black pepper), 1 ounce of allspice berries, and 1 ounce of soda (baking soda). Dissolve all except the peppers and spice in the water; boil in an iron pot and skim as long as any sediment arises. When done add the peppers and the spice after having tied them up in a piece of thin cloth. Stir frequently with a wooden paddle until cool; then pour it over the meat.

In winter the brine need not be boiled. Weigh down as usual. If bacon is desired the sides should remain in the pickle from four to six weeks; hams and shoulders from six to eight weeks; after which they are removed from the brine, washed off and smoked.

**CORNING BEEF NO. 1**
Cut the beef in small pieces, as nearly possible of the same size, say five or six inches square. Weigh out the meat, and for every 100 lbs. allow 8 lbs. of salt. Sprinkle a layer of salt one-fourth of an inch thick on the bottom of the barrel; pack the cuts of meats in as closely as possible, making a layer five or six inches in thickness. Then put on a layer of salt, then a layer of meat in the same way until the barrel is as full as desired. Put a good layer of salt on top and let stand overnight.

Now, for every 100 lbs. of meat add 4 lbs. of sugar, 2 ounces of baking soda, and 4 ounces of saltpeter dissolved in a gallon of tepid water. Three gallons more of water should be sufficient to cover this quantity. Weigh down, and observe the same rules given for pork regarding the cleanliness of barrels, etc.

Watch the brine closely in hot weather, as it is likely to spoil at any time. If the brine appears ropy or does not drip from the fingers freely when immersed, it should be turned off, the meat washed, replaced in the barrel, and new brine added. The sugar or molasses causes this fermentation.

It requires from 28 to 40 days to secure thorough corning.

## CORNING BEEF NO. 2
Cut and pack in a barrel the same as for No. 1, rubbing the salt mixture thoroughly into the meat. Let drain for a few hours. Prepare a brine as follows: For every 100 lbs. of meat use 7 lbs. of salt, 1 ounce each of saltpeter and cayenne pepper, 1 quart of molasses and 8 gallons of salt water. Boil and skim, and when cold pour over the meat. The pepper should be mixed with the salt used in rubbing the meat.

## CAUTION RESPECTING THE BRINE
1. It must be strong enough with salt to float a fresh egg, not an old stale one; an old egg will float in clear water.

2. Use no more saltpeter than is recommended, as it is a powerful astringent and hardens the muscles of the meat, making it inferior. In cold weather use just one-half the amount or none.

3. In warm weather do not forget to examine the brine twice per week, and if it is inclined to become ropy, pour off, boil, and skim thoroughly, cool, and pour over the meat, or make a new brine altogether.

## CAUTION RESPECTING THE BARRELS OR CONTAINERS
1. As has been said before, the vessels in which you wish to pickle your meat must be clean.

2. Do not take meat from a container and immediately fill it again with fresh meat until it has been thoroughly cleansed and made sweet.

3. Do not attempt to use a vessel in which meat has spoiled until it has been thoroughly cleansed, with no trace of the taint left. See that it is well sterilized.

4. Do not use vessels for pork in which beef has been pickled, neither beef in vessels in which pork has been pickled.

**CAUTION RESPECTING THE MEAT**
1. Use only good, clean, sweet meat that has been carried through the chilling process.

2. If meat has begun to taint or sour, be it ever so little, do not attempt to pickle it, as it will continue to taint and spoil the entire contents of the container.

**SMOKING**
Smoking adds much to the flavor and palatability of both pickled and dry meats, besides acting in some degree as a preservative and protection against insects.

**THE HOUSE**
Where much meat is to be smoked, a house 9 or 10 feet high is the most desirable. It should be built very tight so as to keep the smoke in. There should be several ventilators at the top sufficient to insure a draft that will carry the smoke out slowly.

The meat should be hung 6 or 7 feet from the bottom of the house. Small amounts can be smoked in large dry goods boxes or over the fire, so that, if it should blaze up unduly, it will not heat the meat directly under it.

**FUEL**
Hard wood of any kind is good for smoking meat, but green maple or hickory, smothered with sawdust of the same material, is the most desirable. Corn cobs make an excellent substitute for hard wood. Do not use pine or resinous woods of any kind; and if the highest quality of meat is desired, do not use soft wood of any kind, not even corn

cobs, as they deposit a great deal of carbon or soot on the meat, making it black and unsightly, as well as injuring the flavor.

The smoking process should continue until the meat has a nice light, smoke brown which will require from three to four days and even longer if the fire is not kept steadily going.

**HEAD CHEESE**
Cut a hog's head into four pieces. Remove the brain, ears, snout, skin, and eyes. Cut off the fattest part for lard. Put the lean and bony parts to soak overnight in cold water to extract the blood, etc. Wash carefully and put over the fire to boil, using water enough to cover it. Boil until the meat separates readily from the bone; then remove from the fire and pick out all the bones. Drain off the liquor, saving a part of it for future use. Chop the meat up finely with a chopping knife.

Return to the kettle, and pour on enough liquor to cover the meat. Let it boil for about half an hour. Season with salt and pepper to taste just before renovating it from the fire.

Turn it into a shallow pan or dish; cover with a piece of cheesecloth, and put on a board with a weight to make it solid. When cold it should be sliced thin, and served without further cooking.

I have given only a few of Dr. Carver's receipts for pickling, curing and preparing meats.

THE END.

www.ingramcontent.com/pod-product-compliance
Lightning Source LLC
Chambersburg PA
CBHW071731080526
44588CB00013B/1981